Mandala Animals Adult Coloring Book

LENKA SARKHELOVA

Copyright © 2018 by Lenka Sarkhelova

First Printing, 2018

ISBN- 9781723832338

INTRODUCTION

Need a relaxing and exciting activity?

Lit up your artistic side and try this Mandala Animals coloring book to brighten up your day the way you want it to look like!

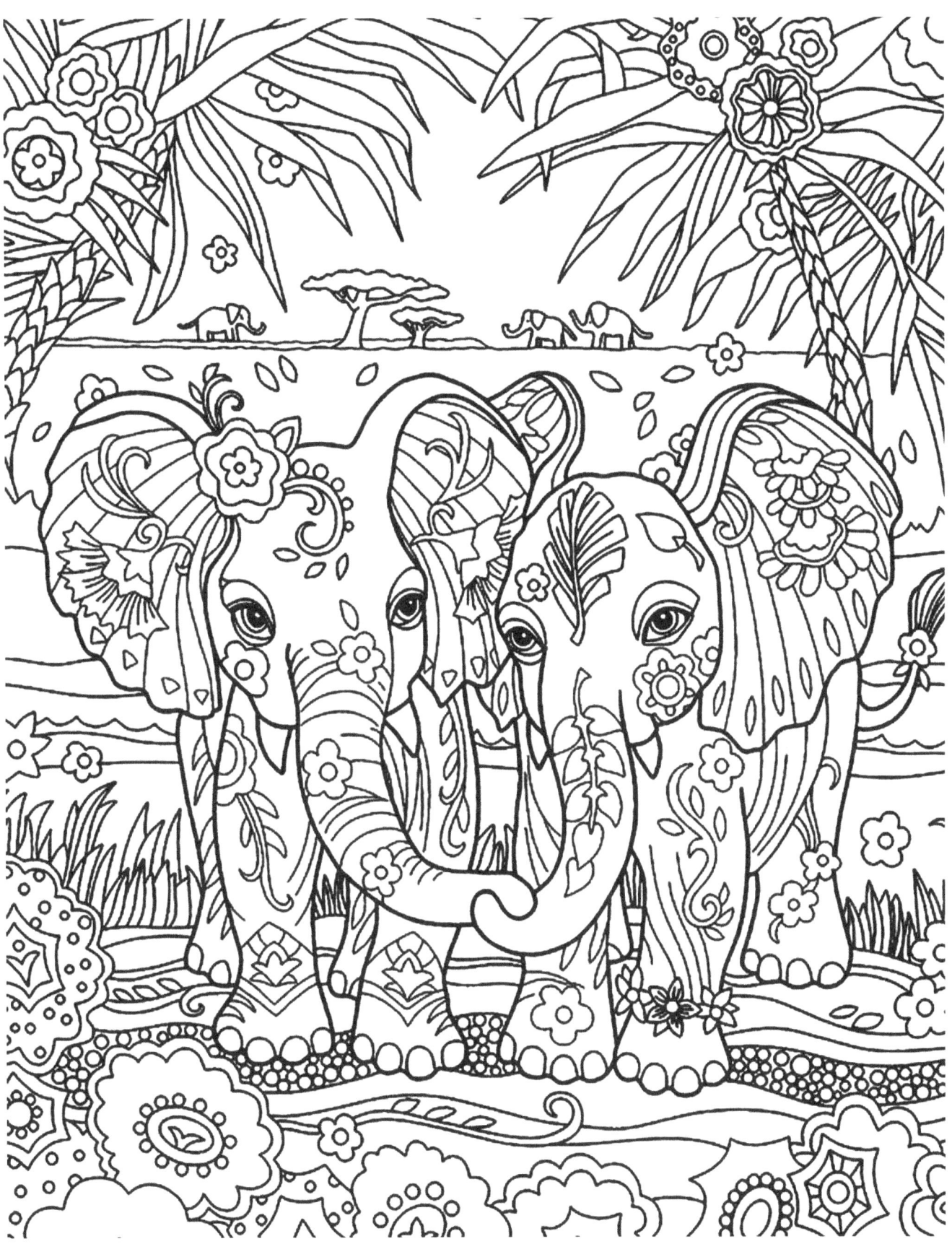

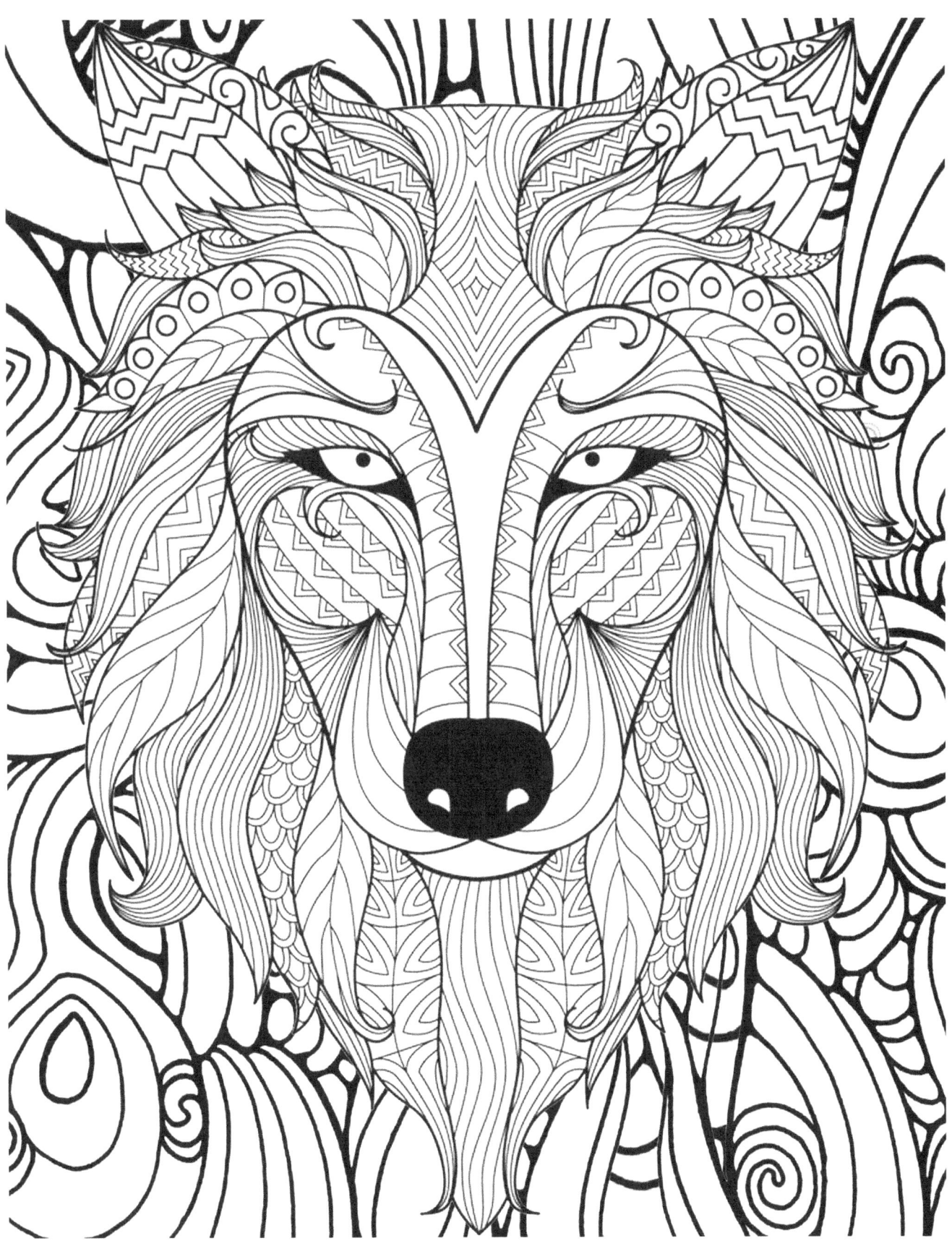

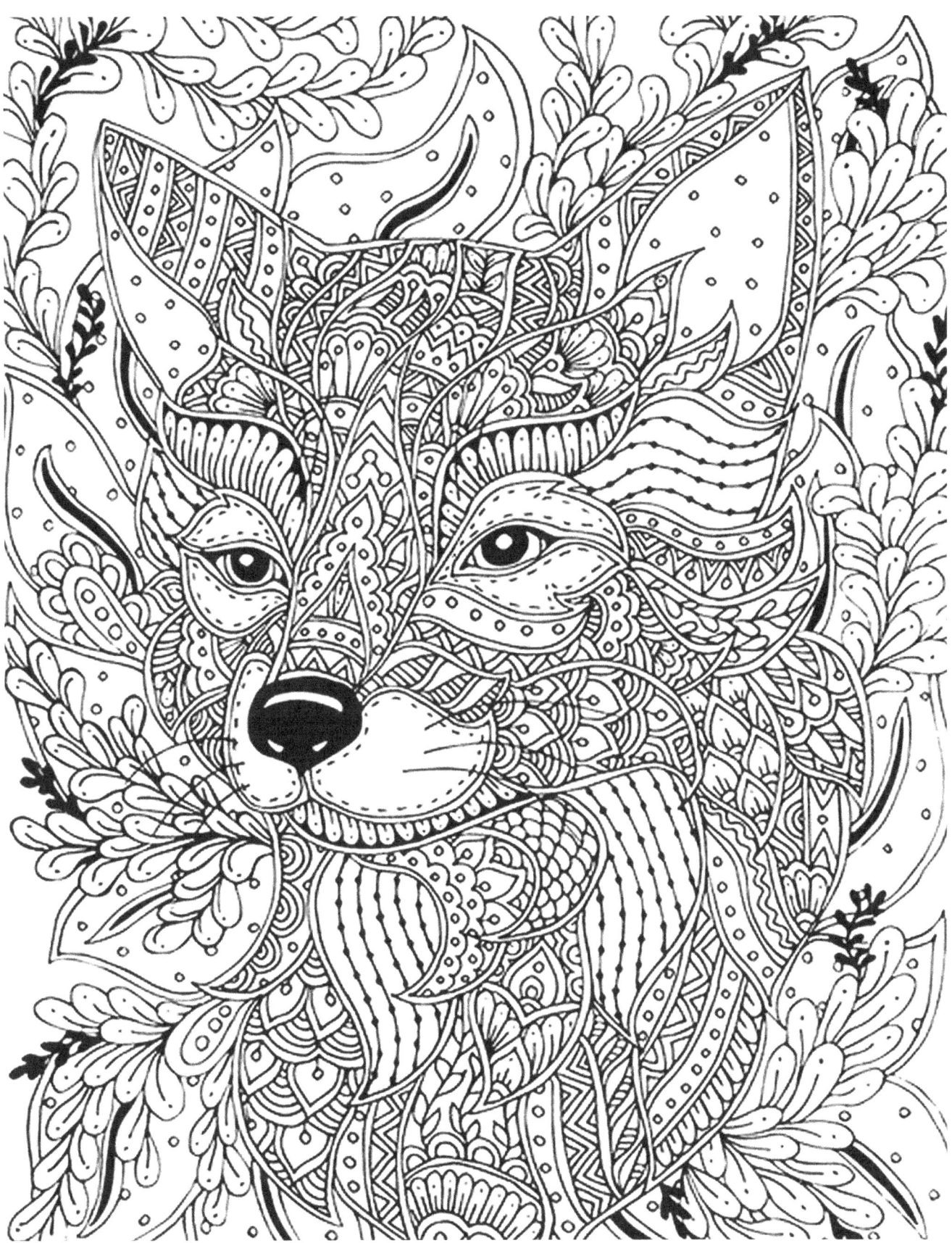

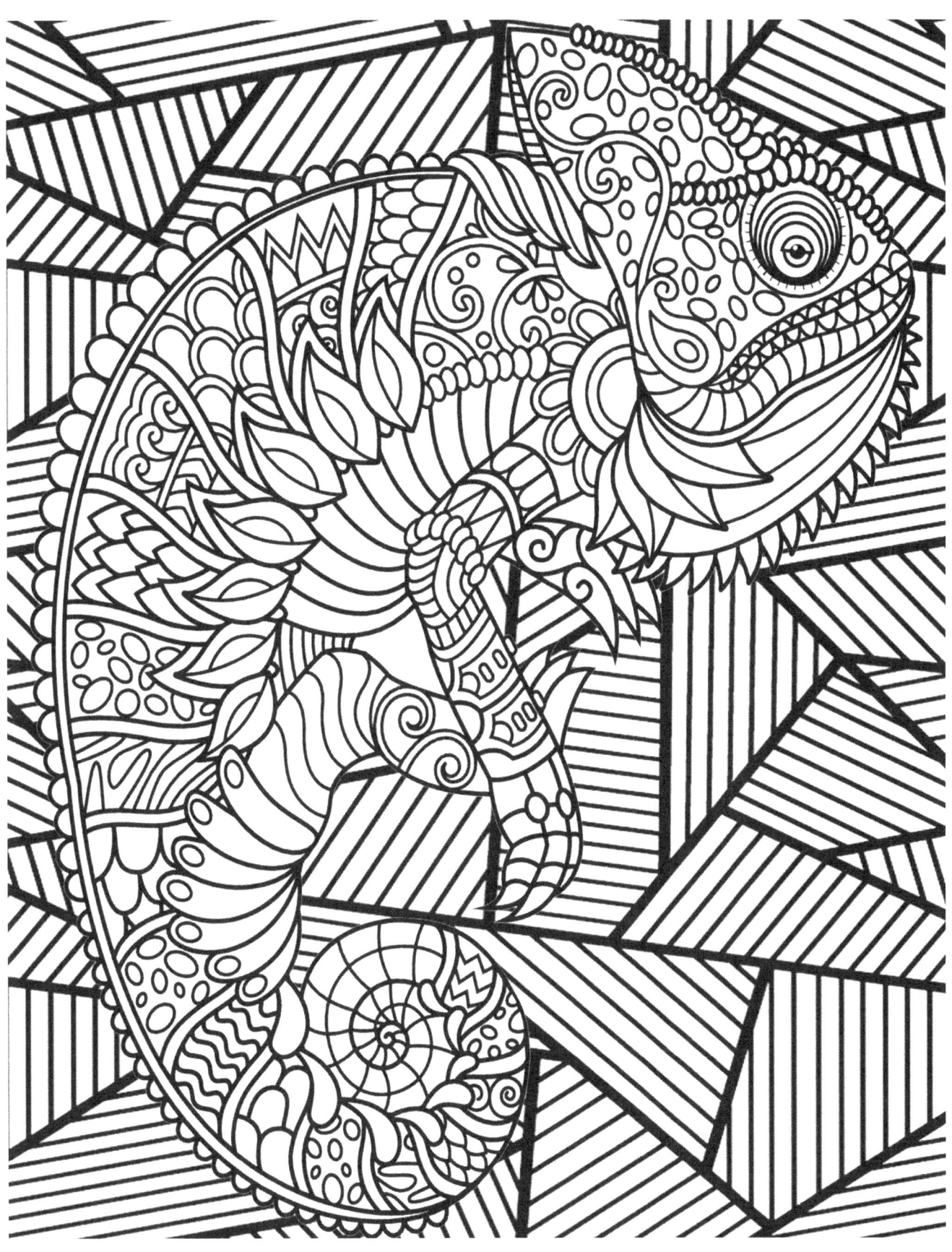

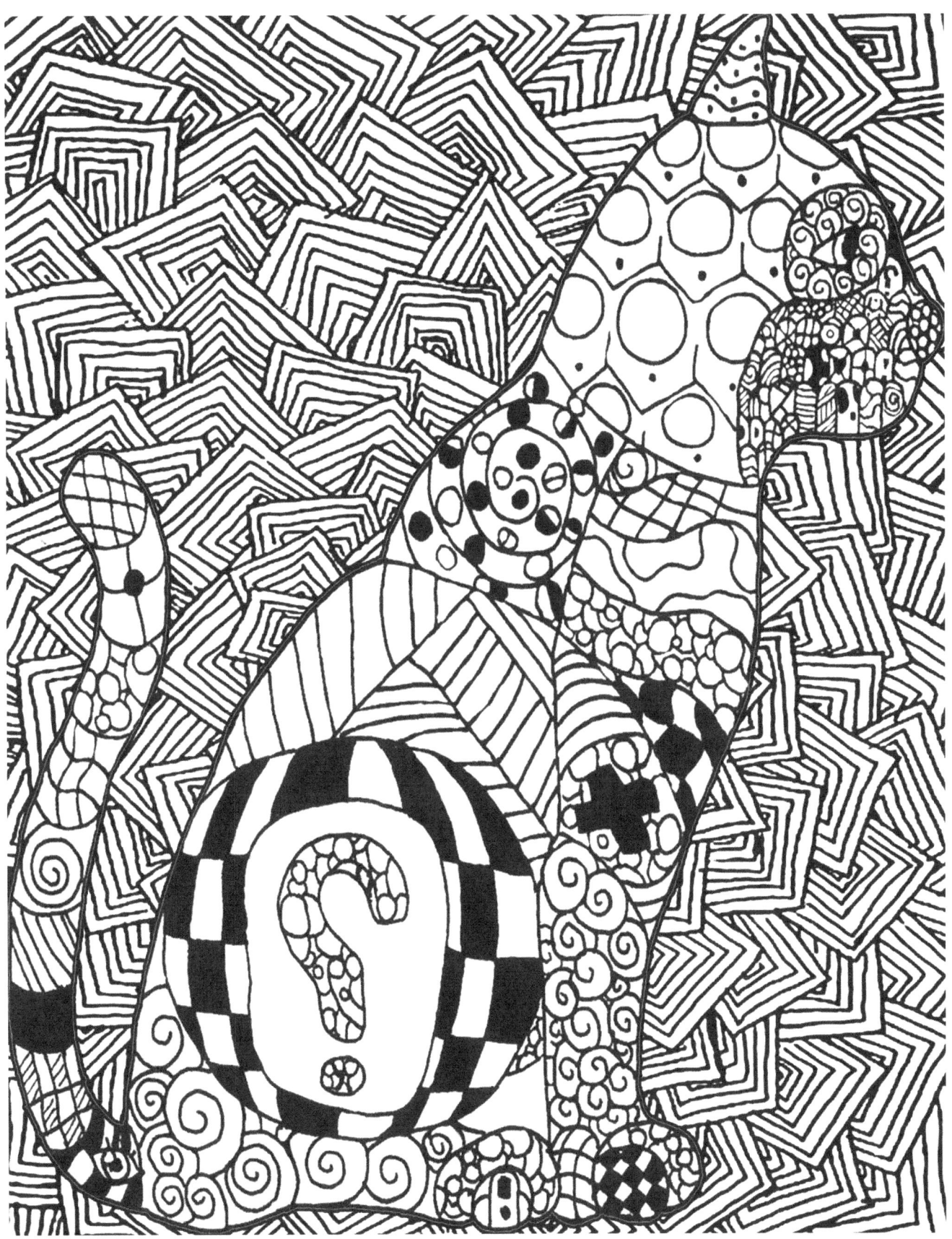

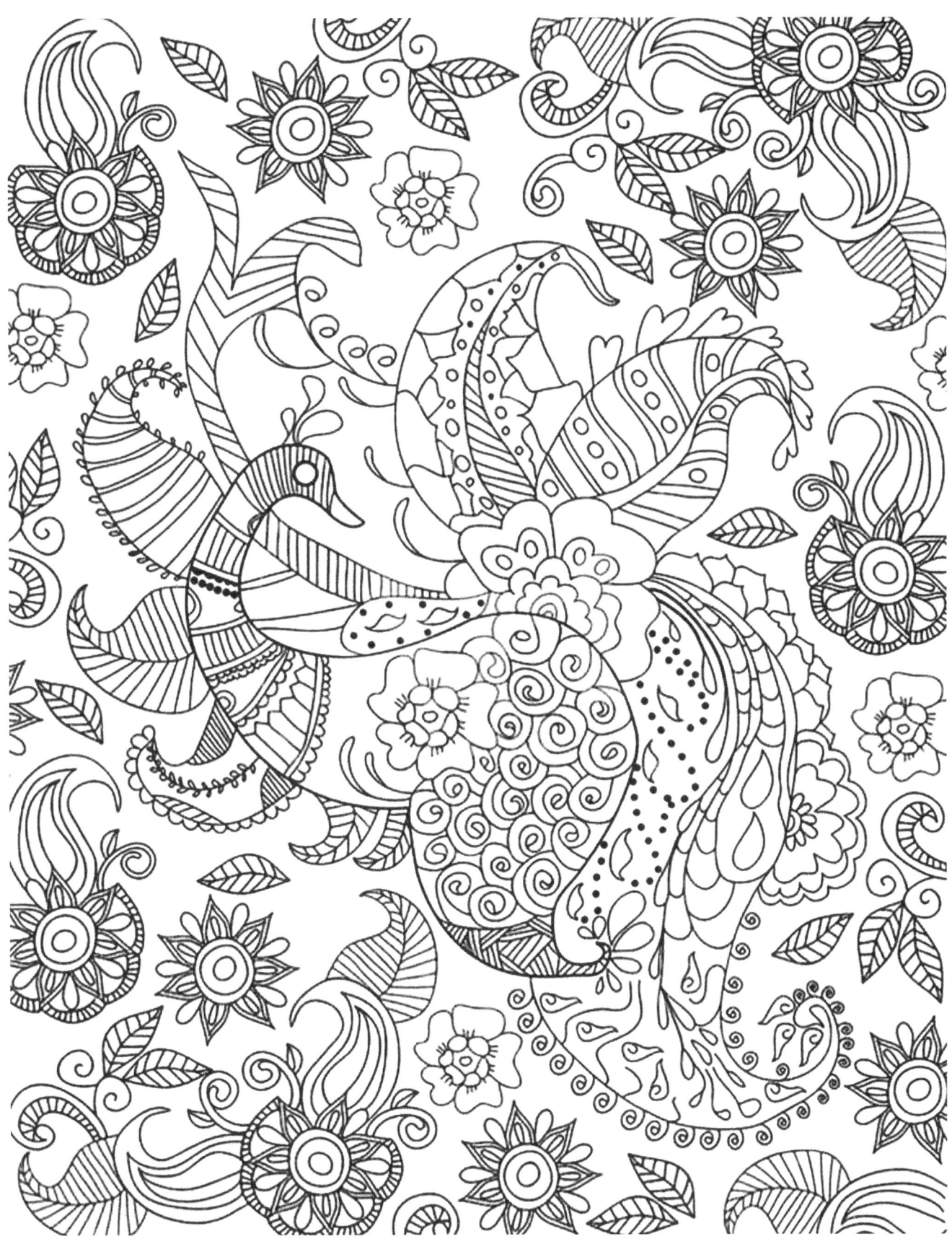

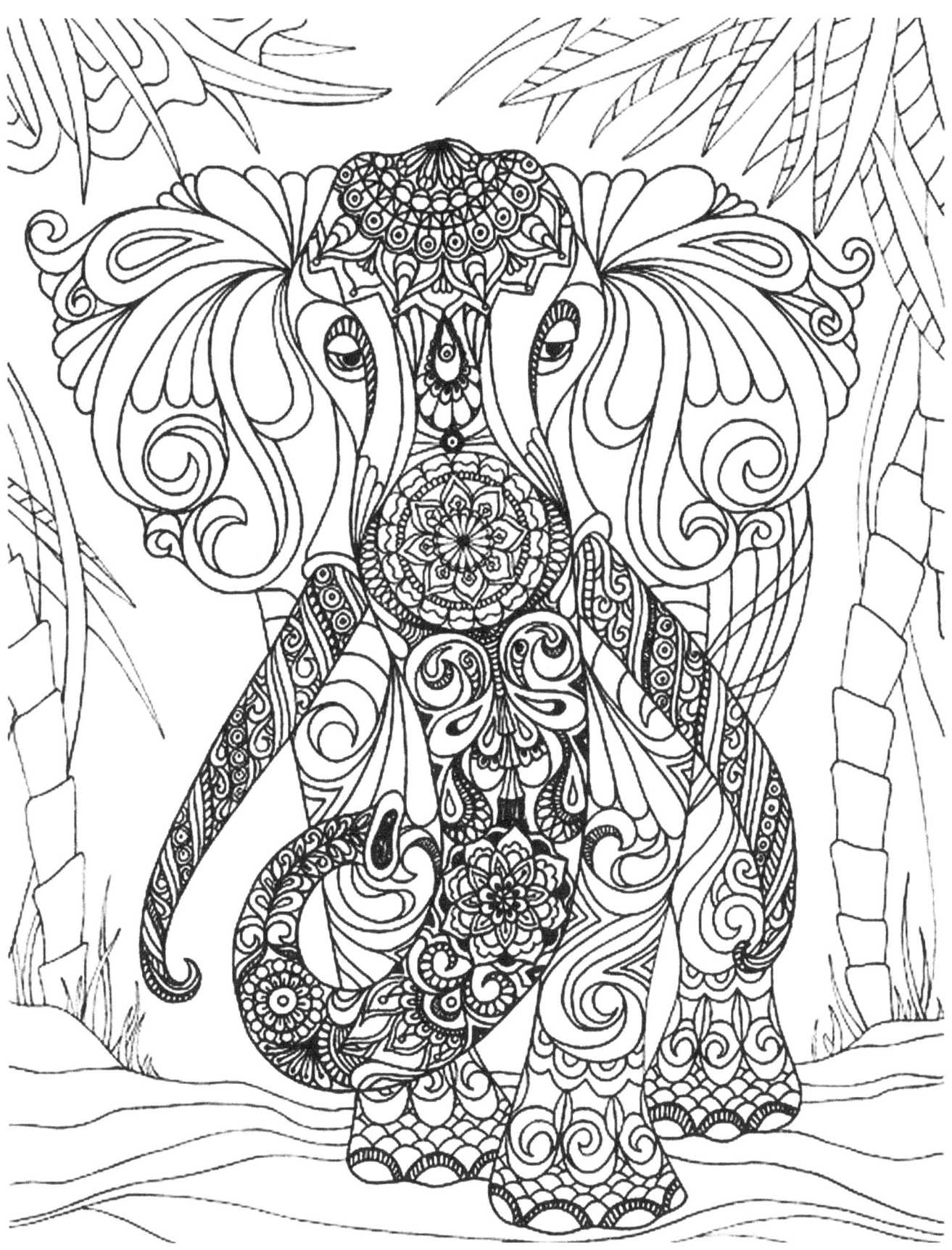

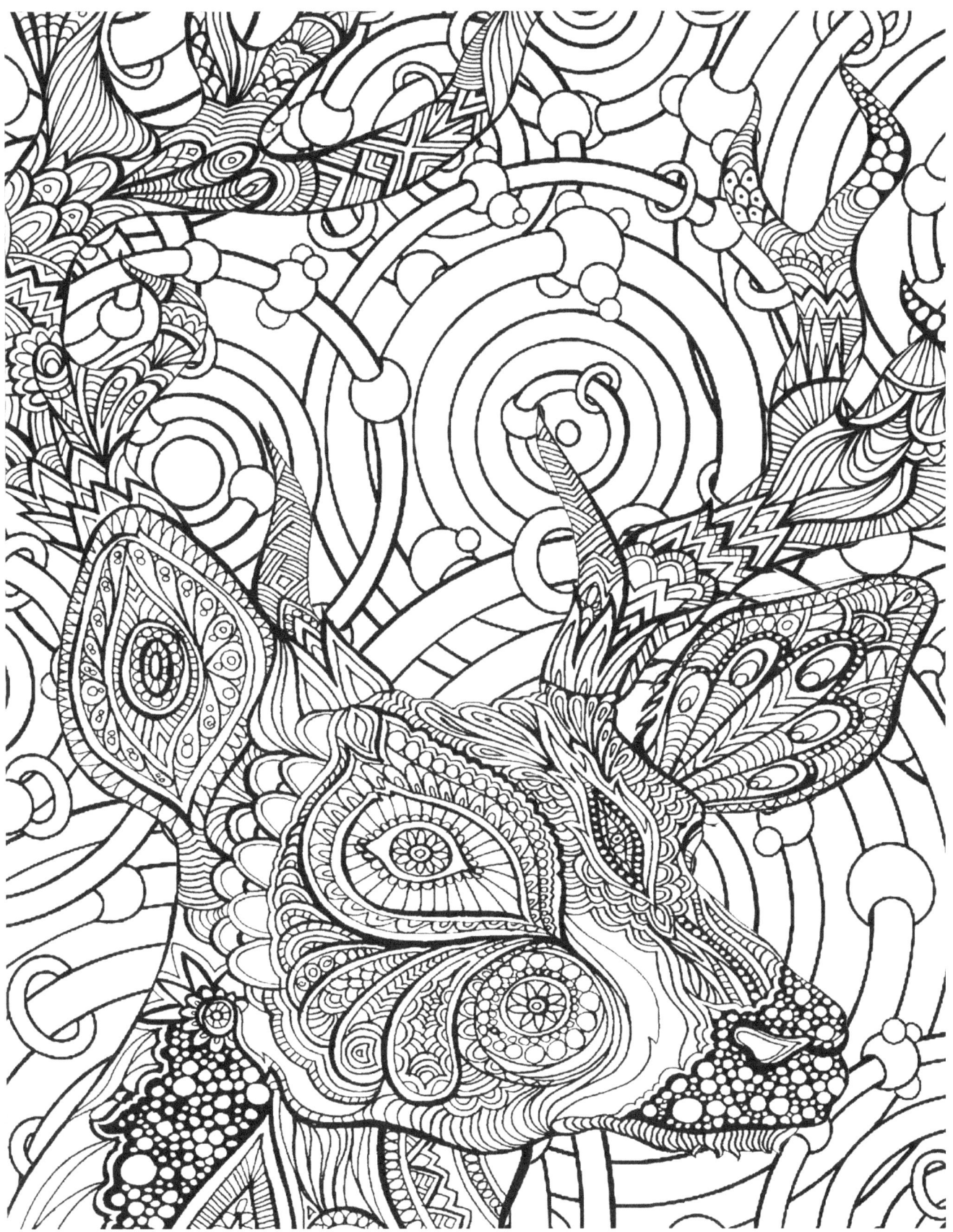

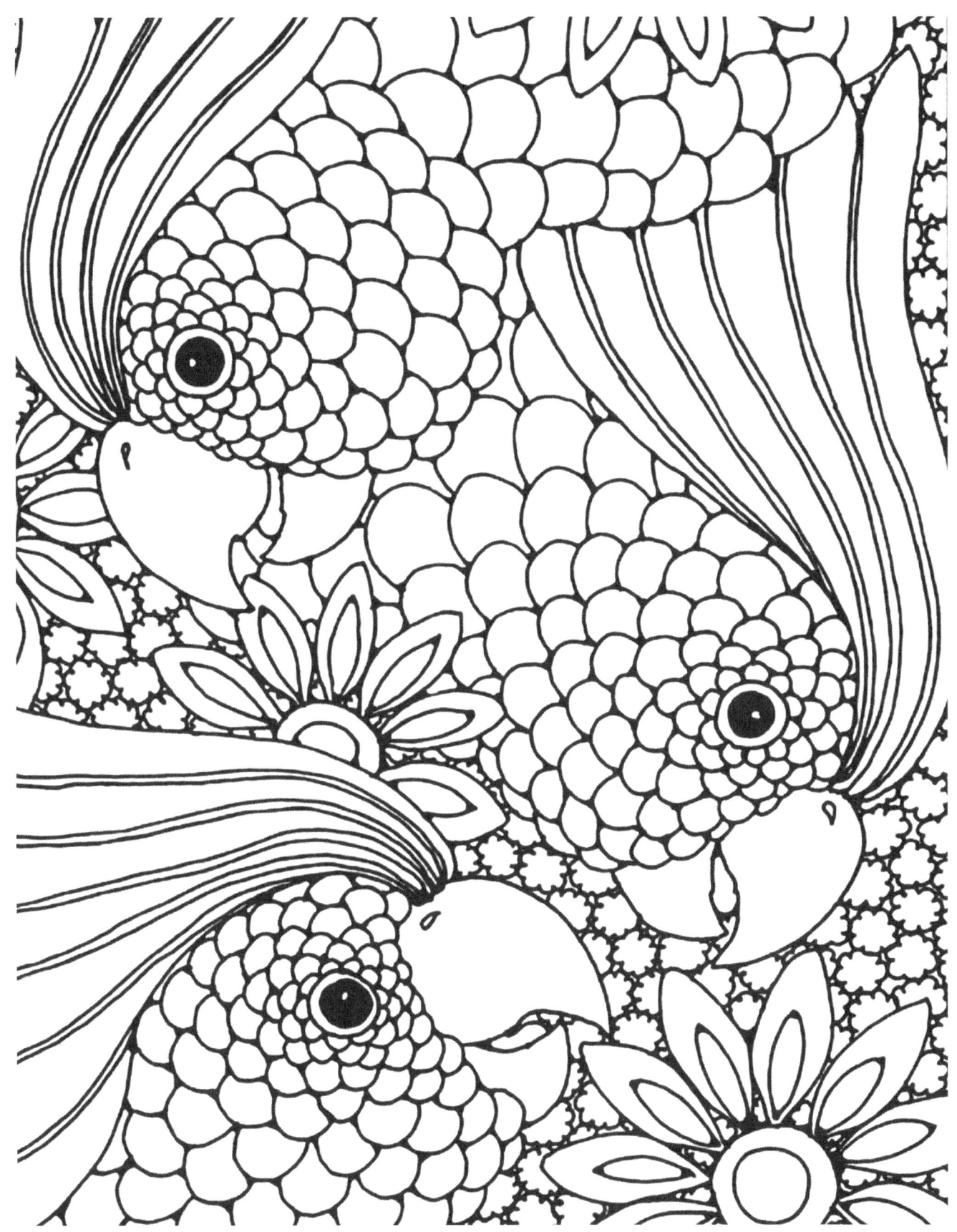

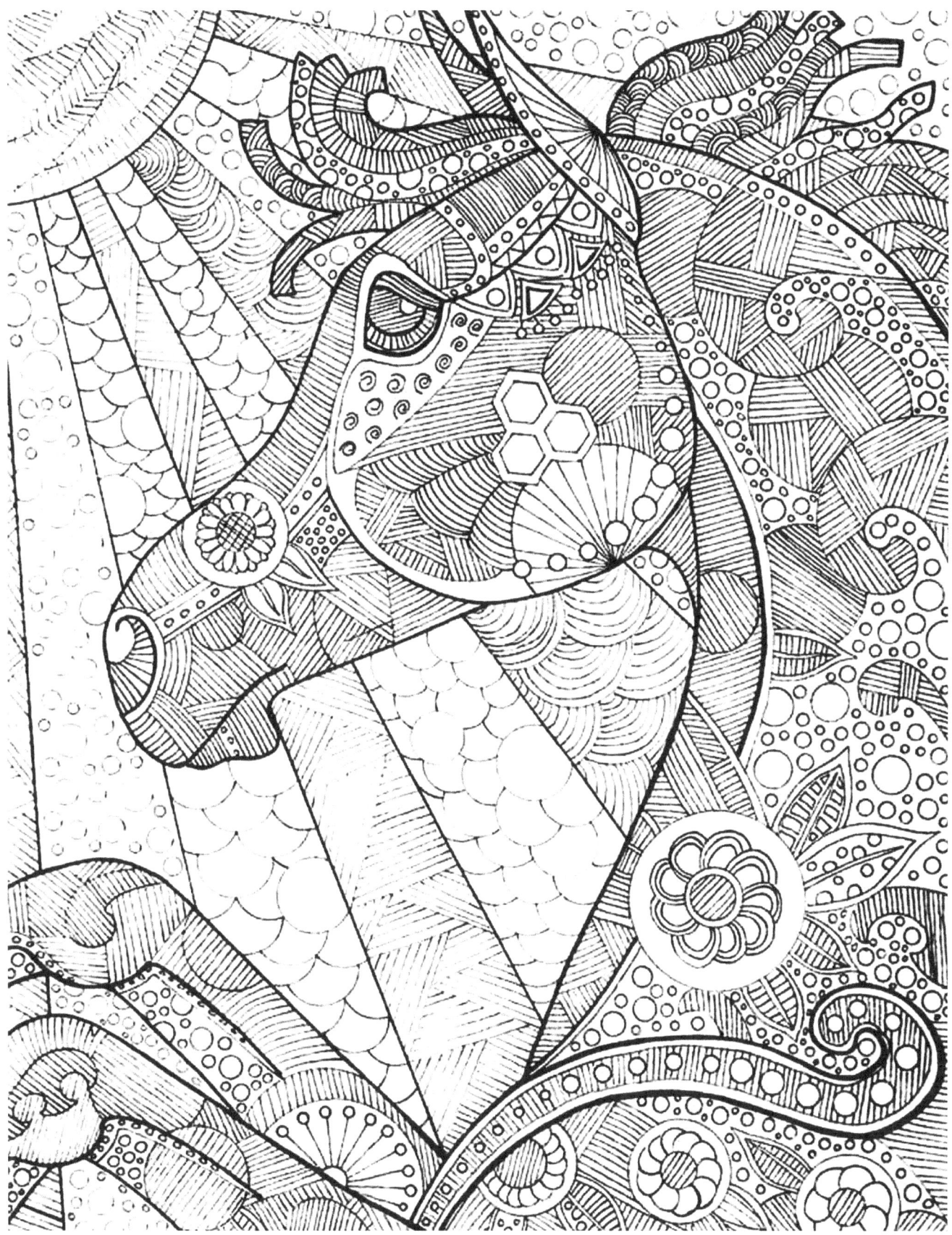

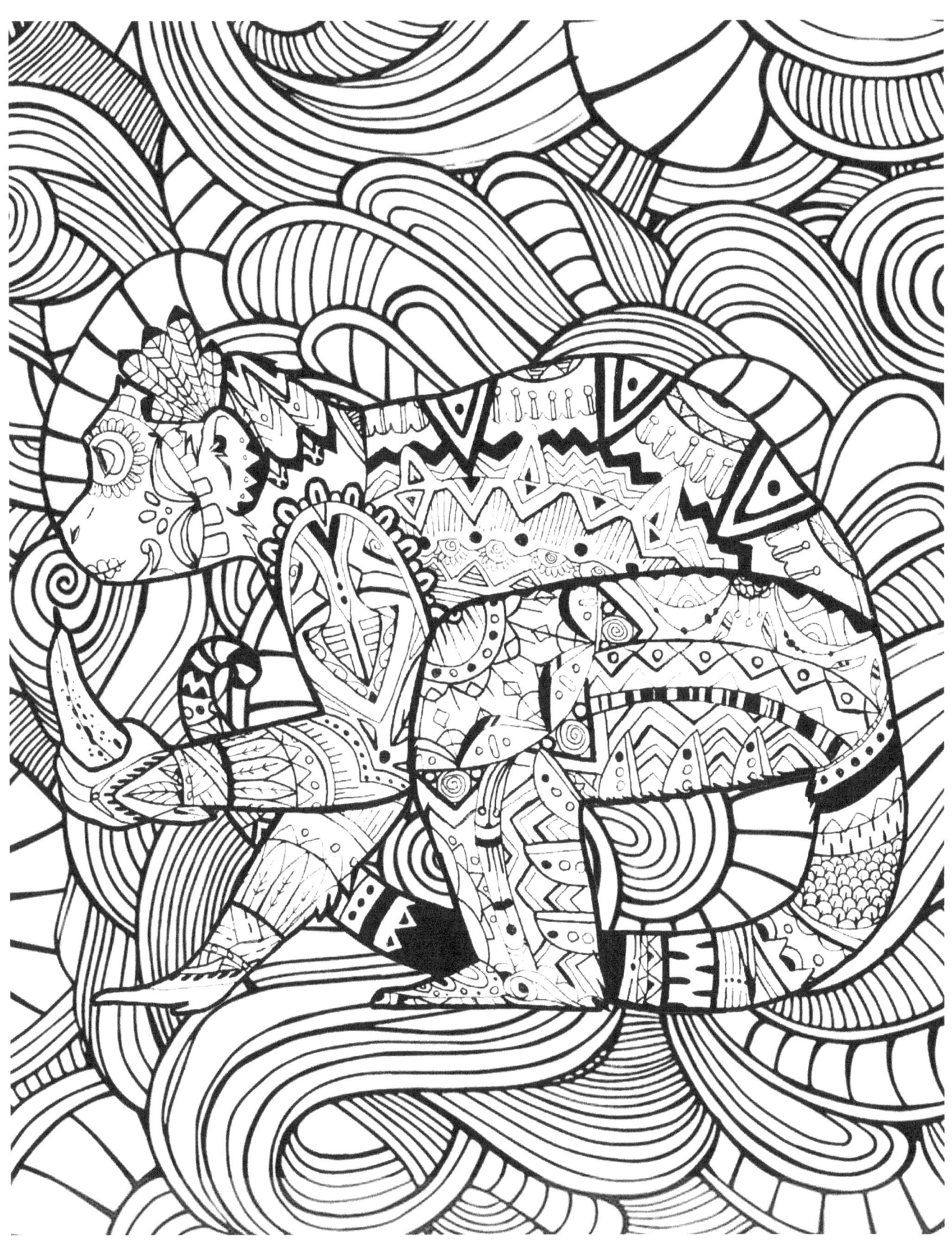

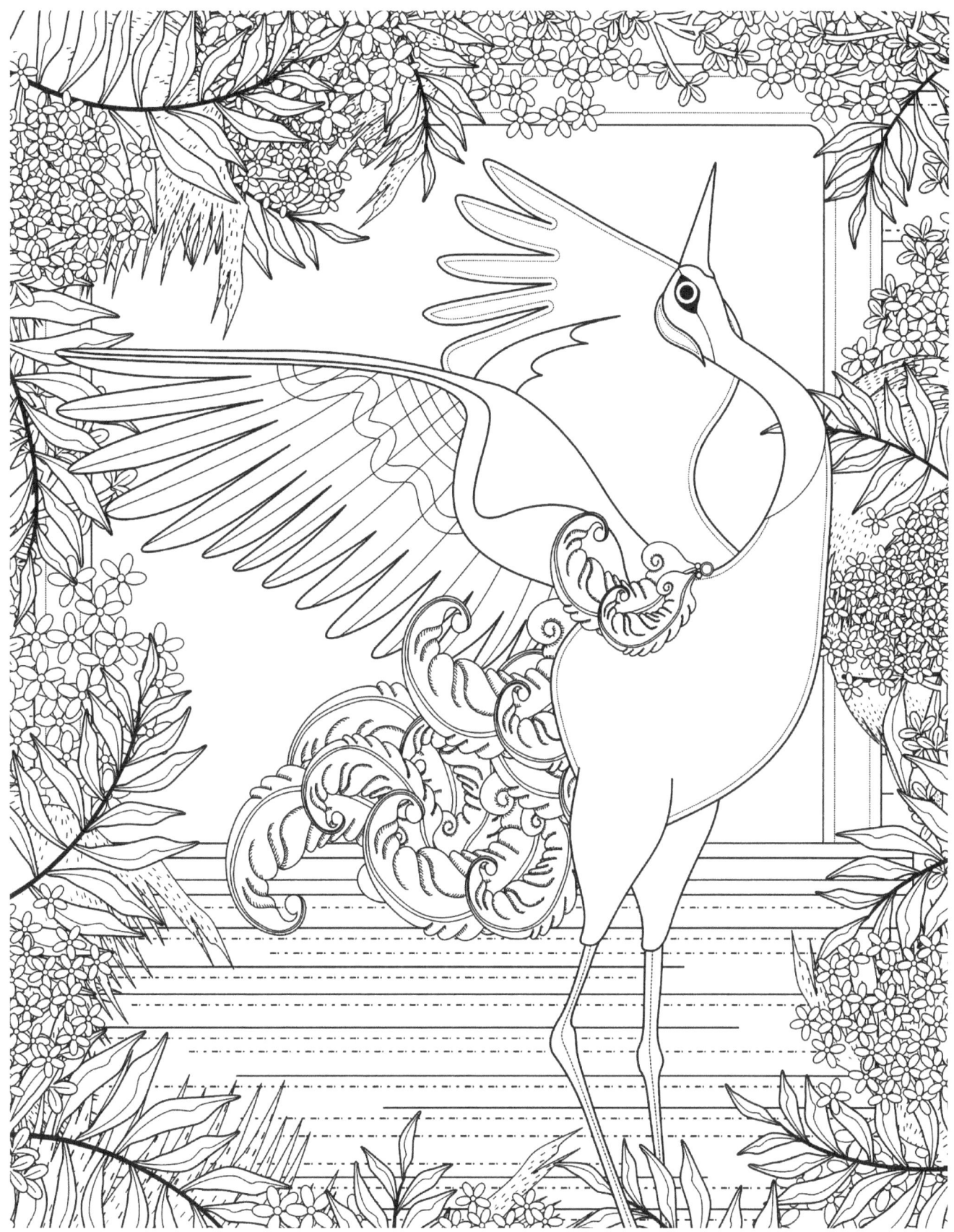

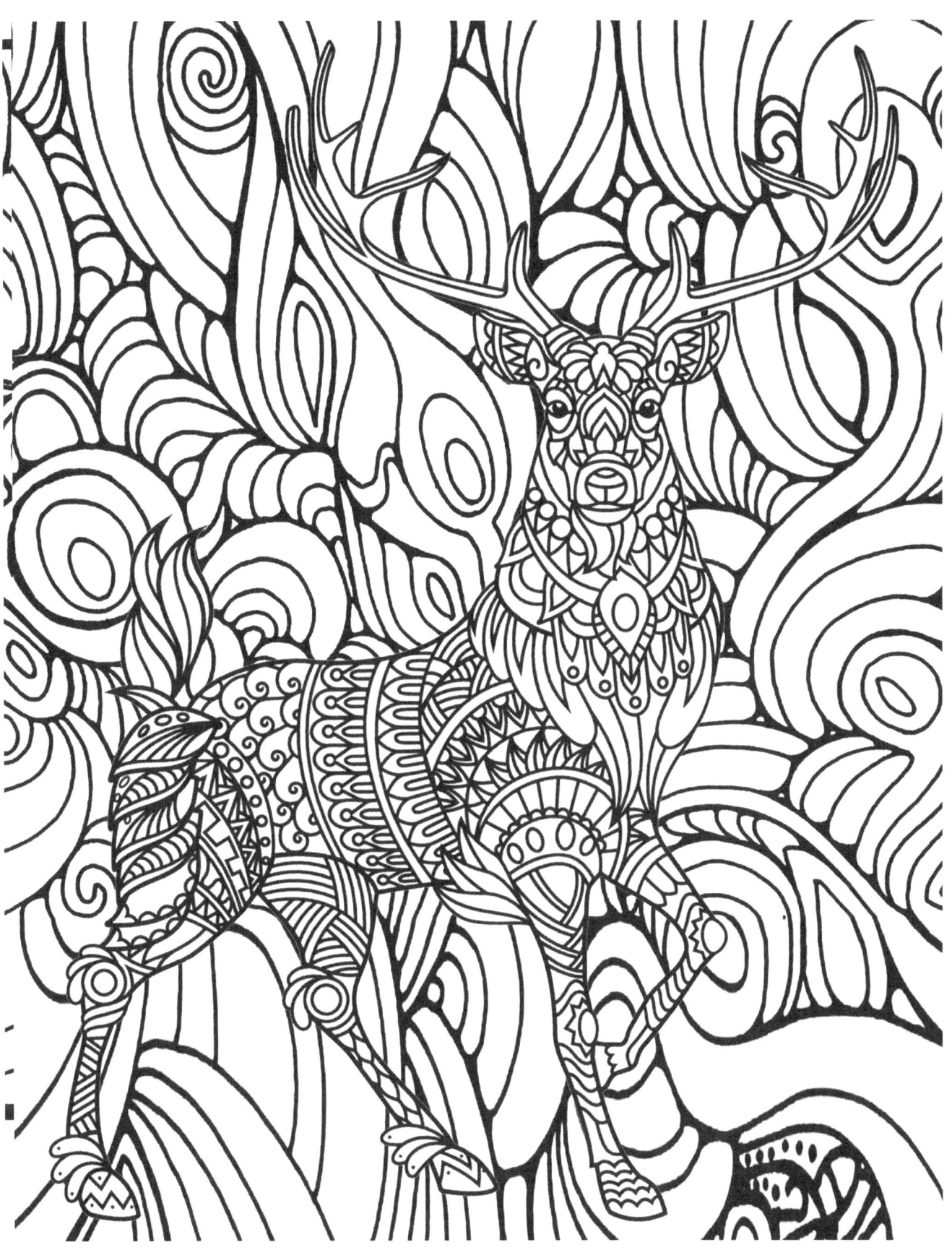

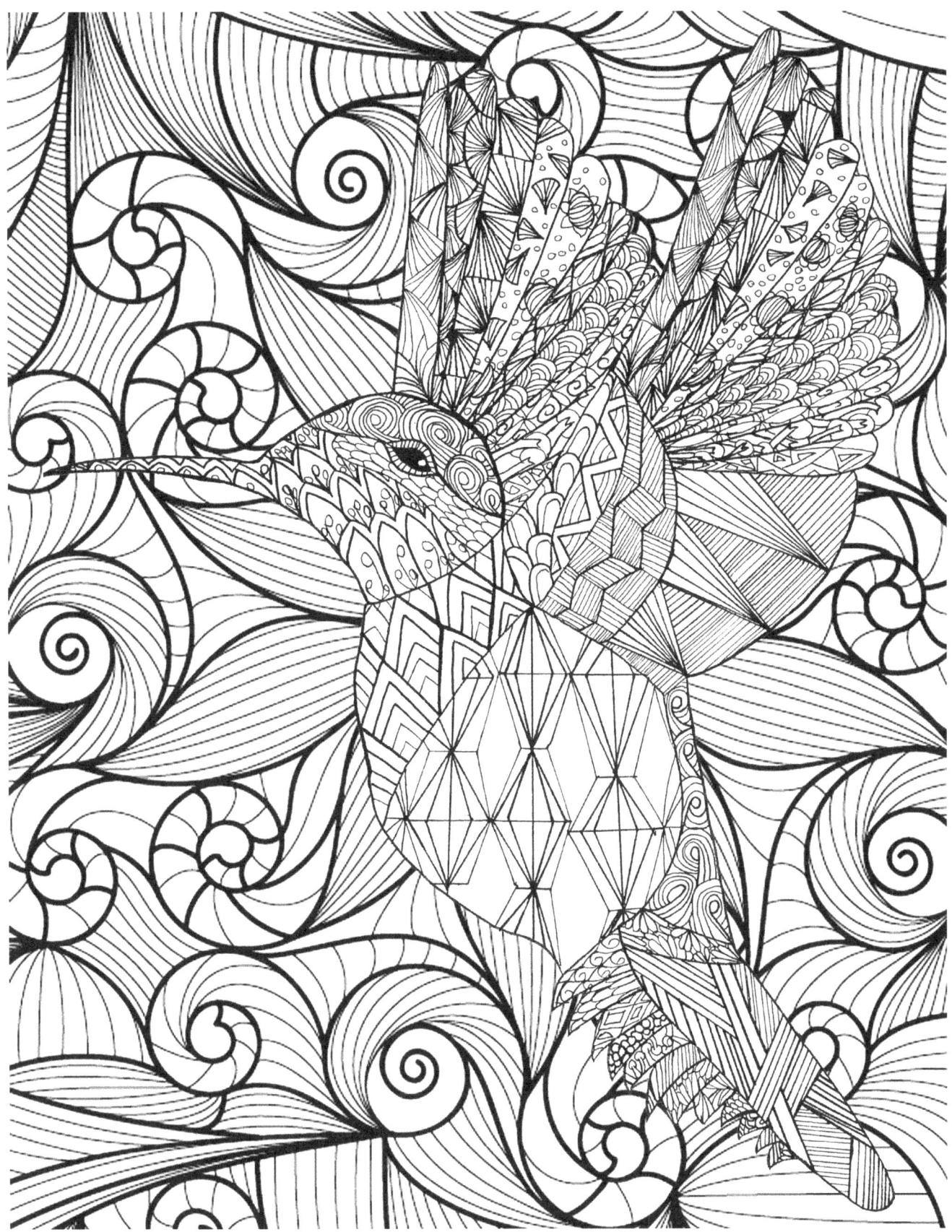

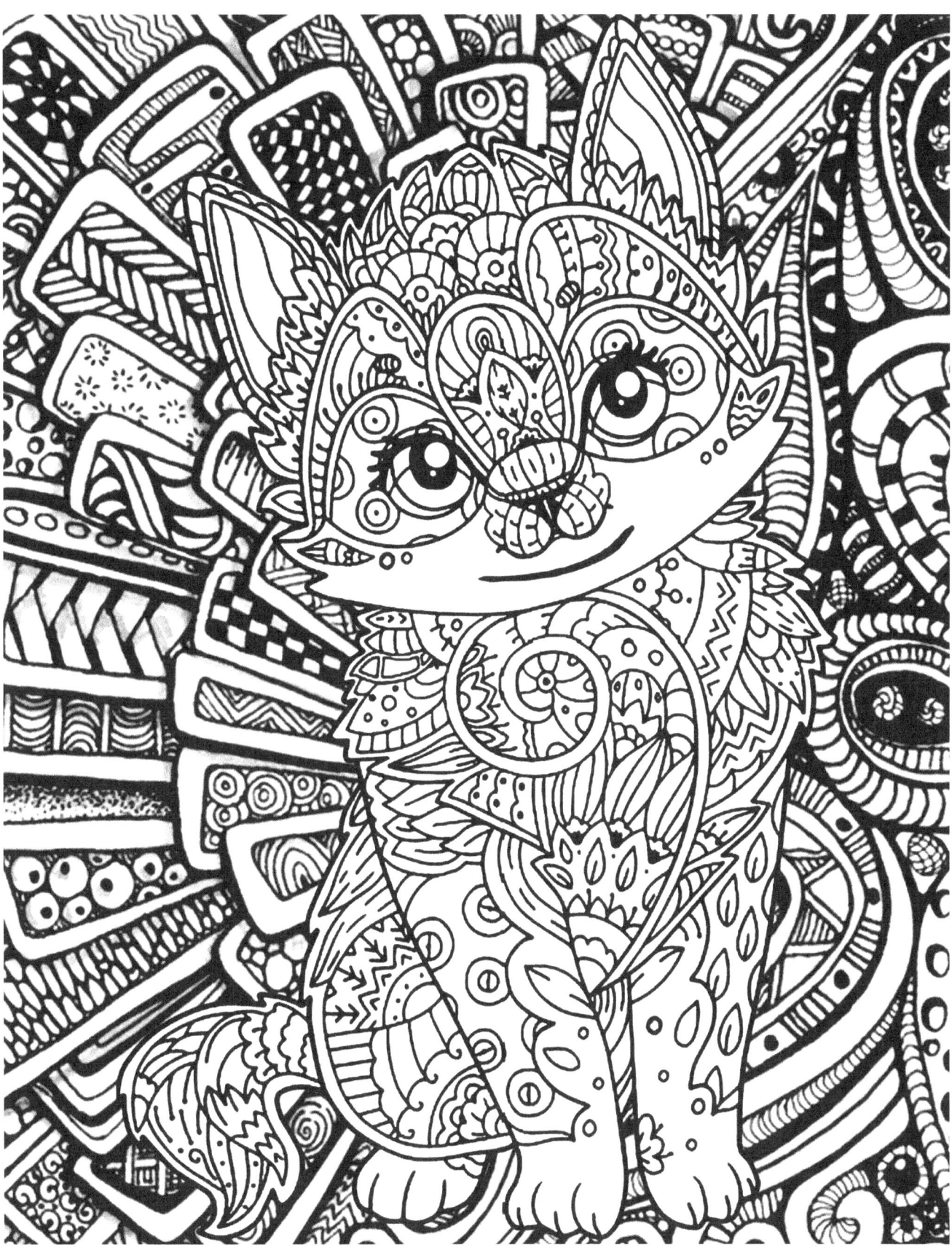

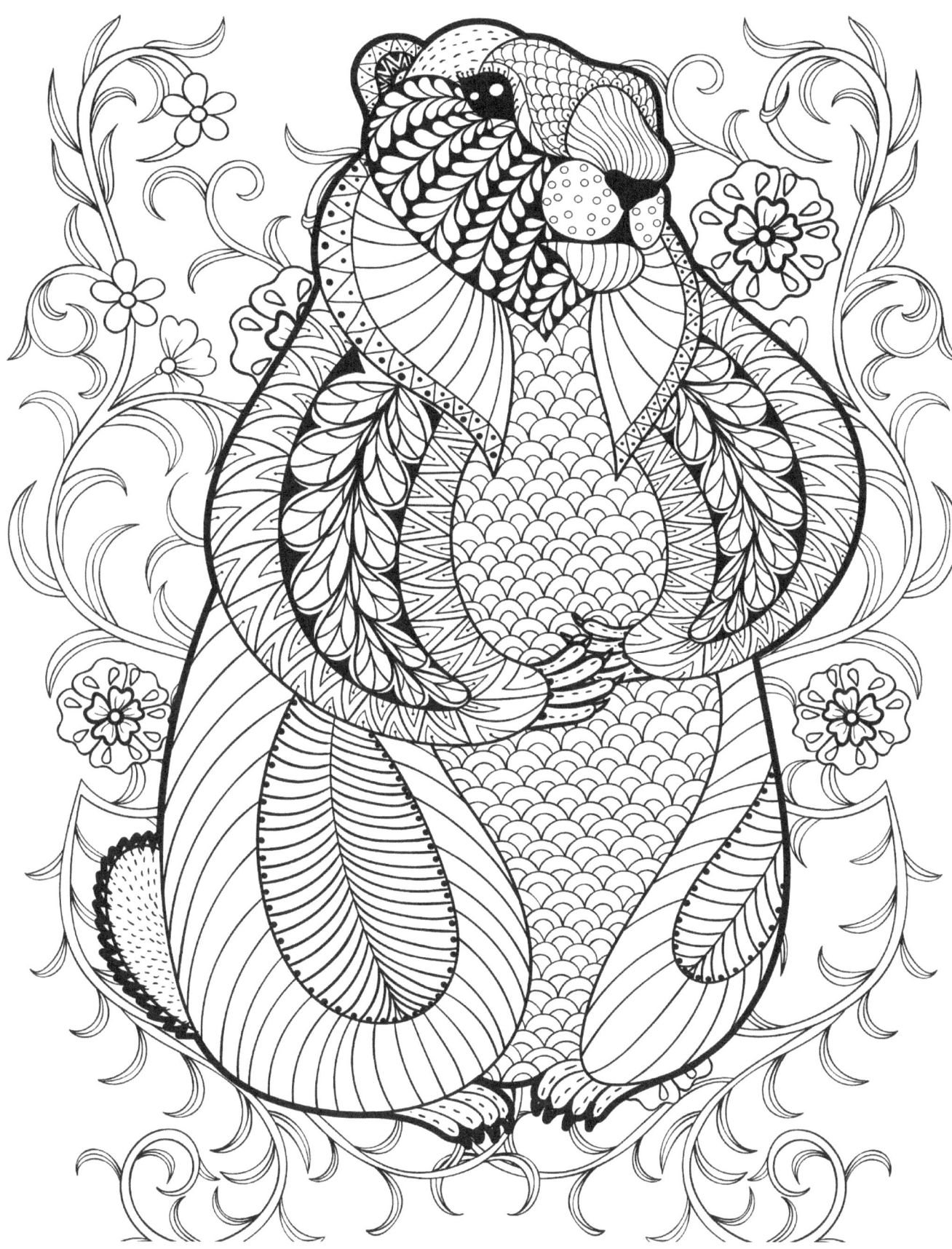

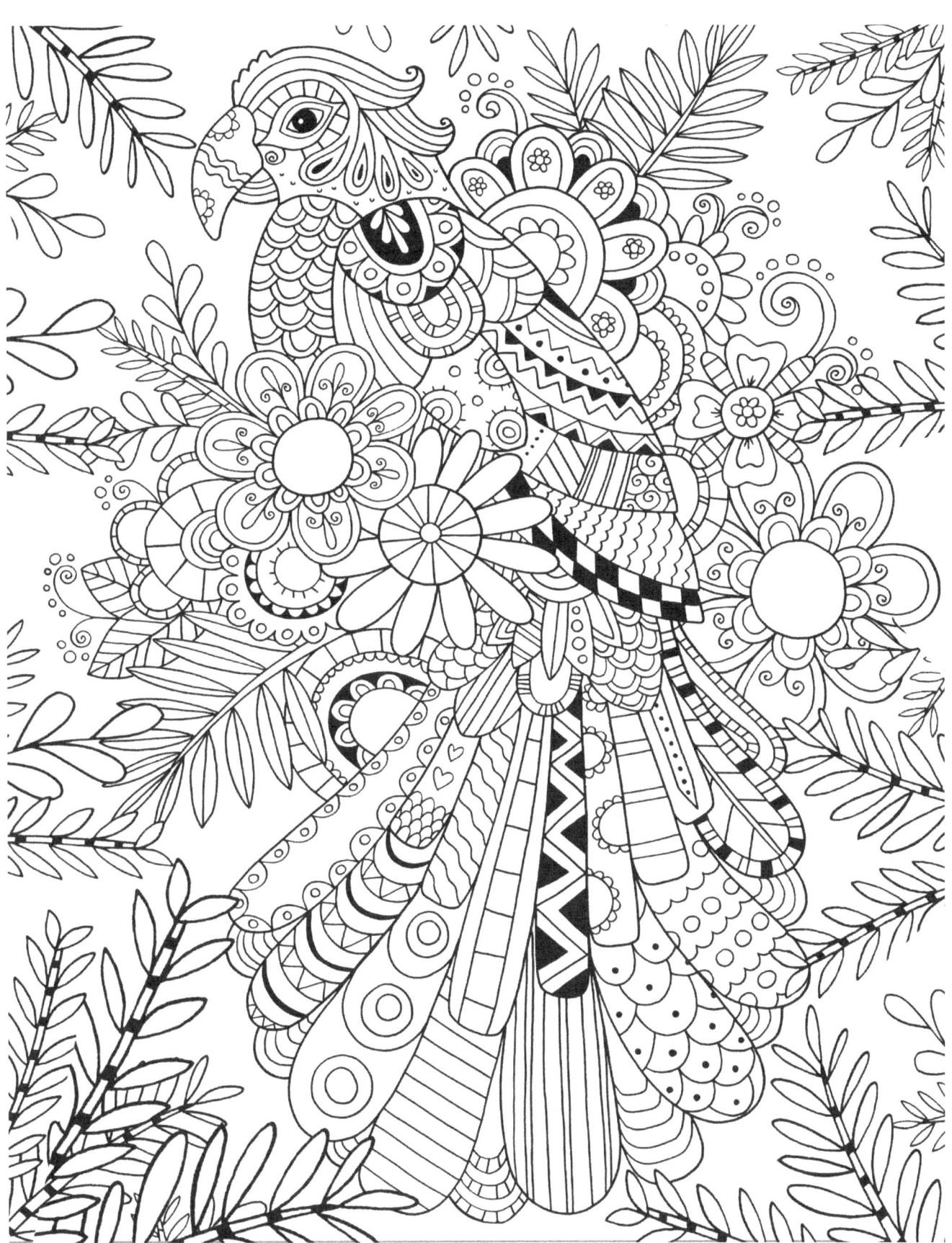

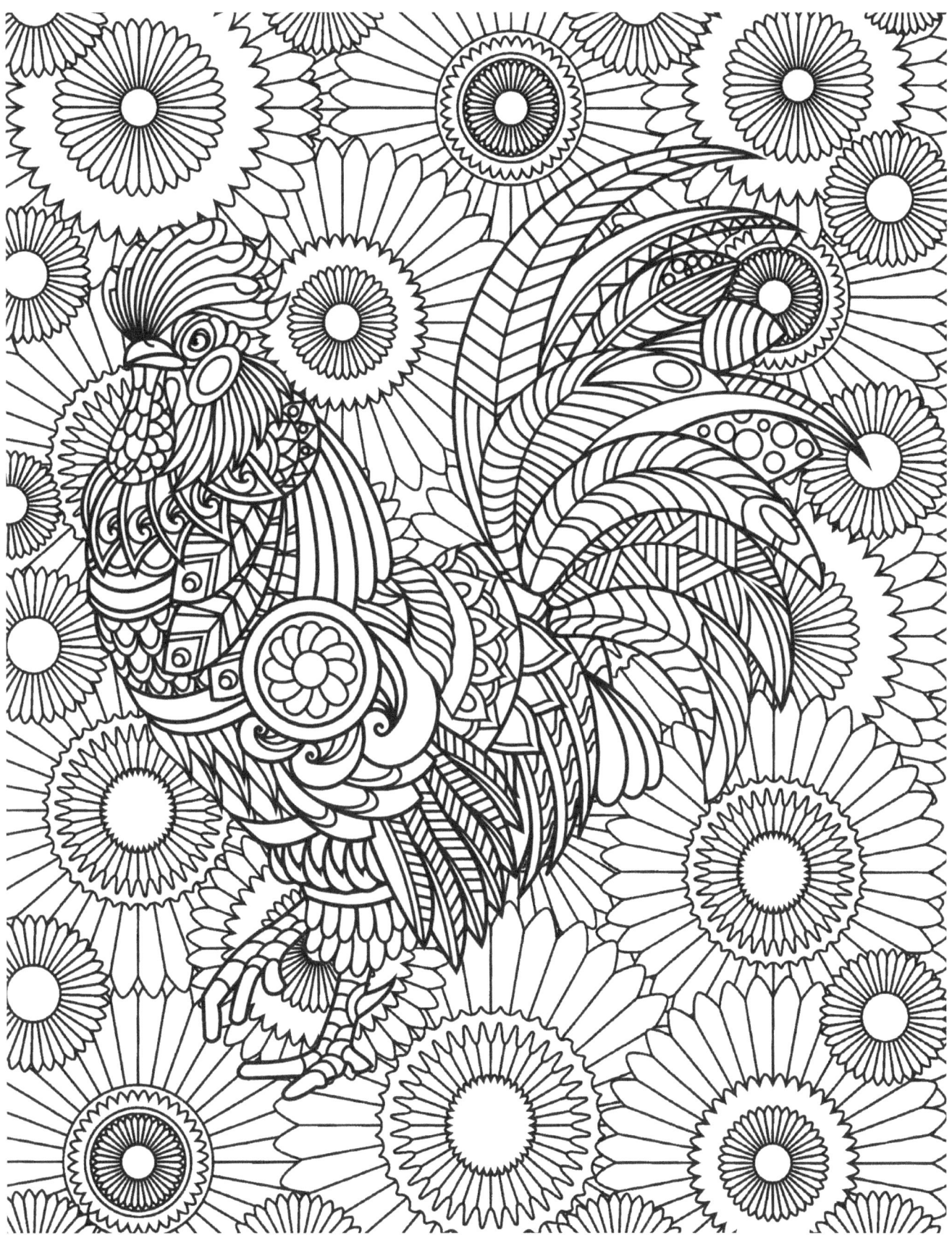

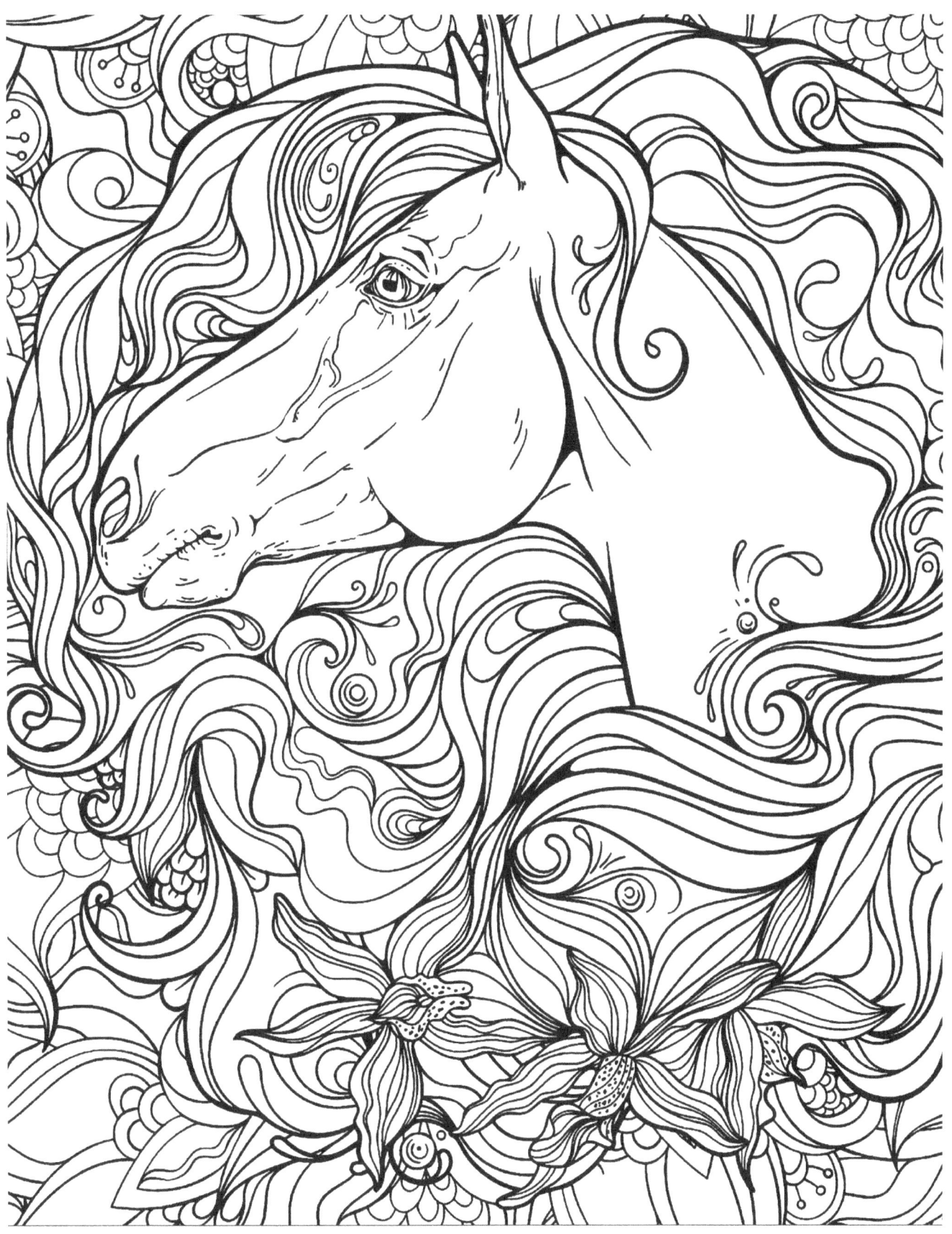

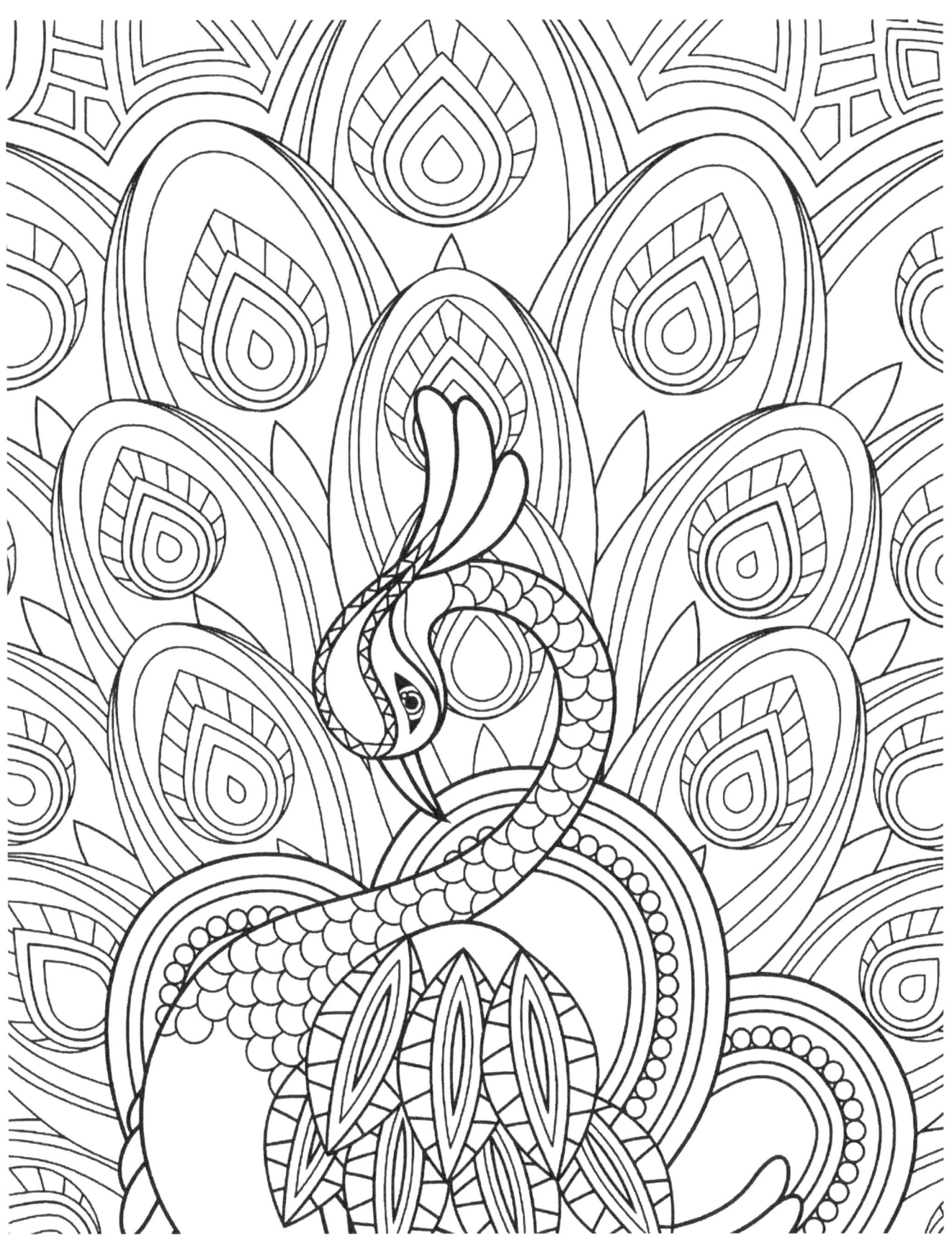

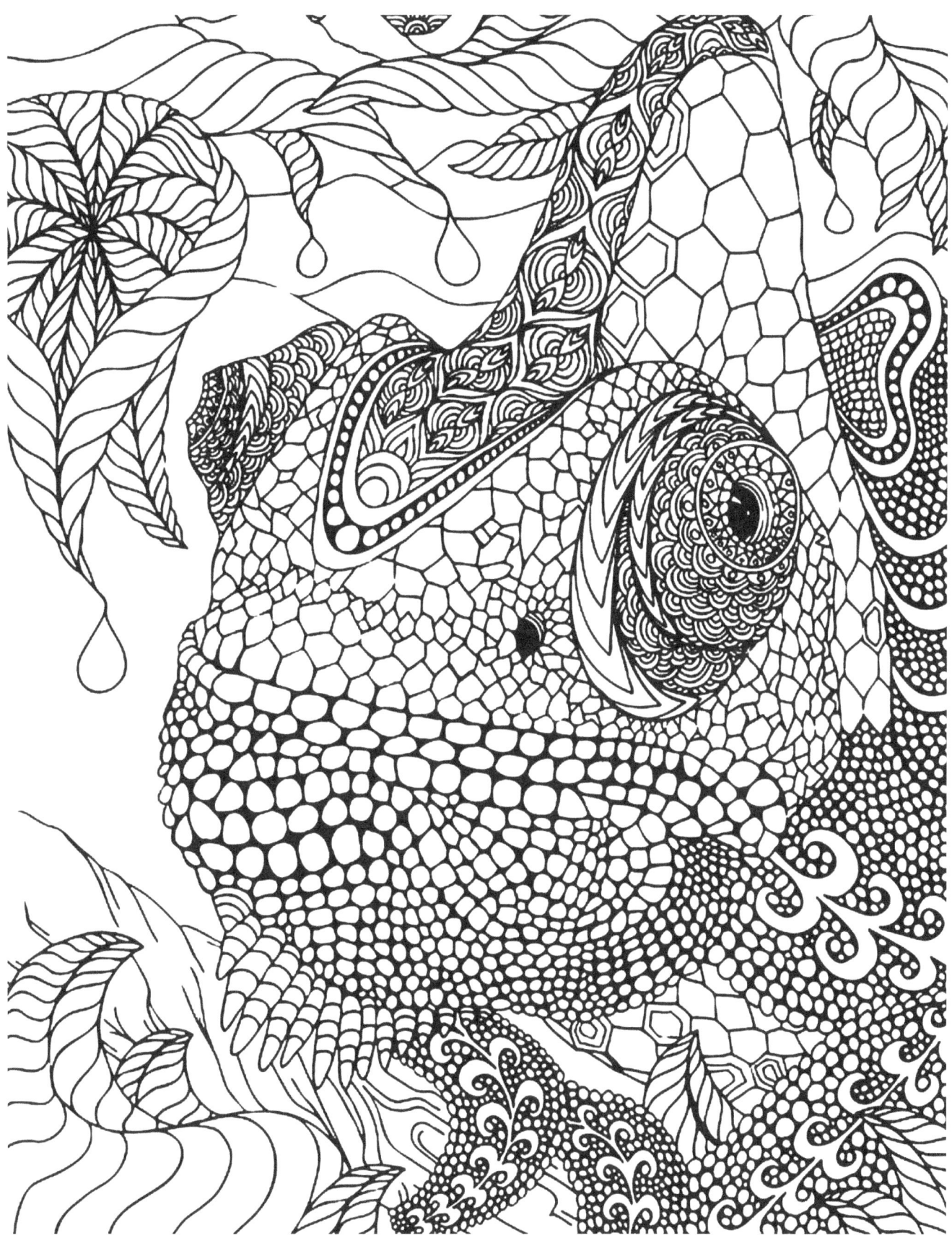

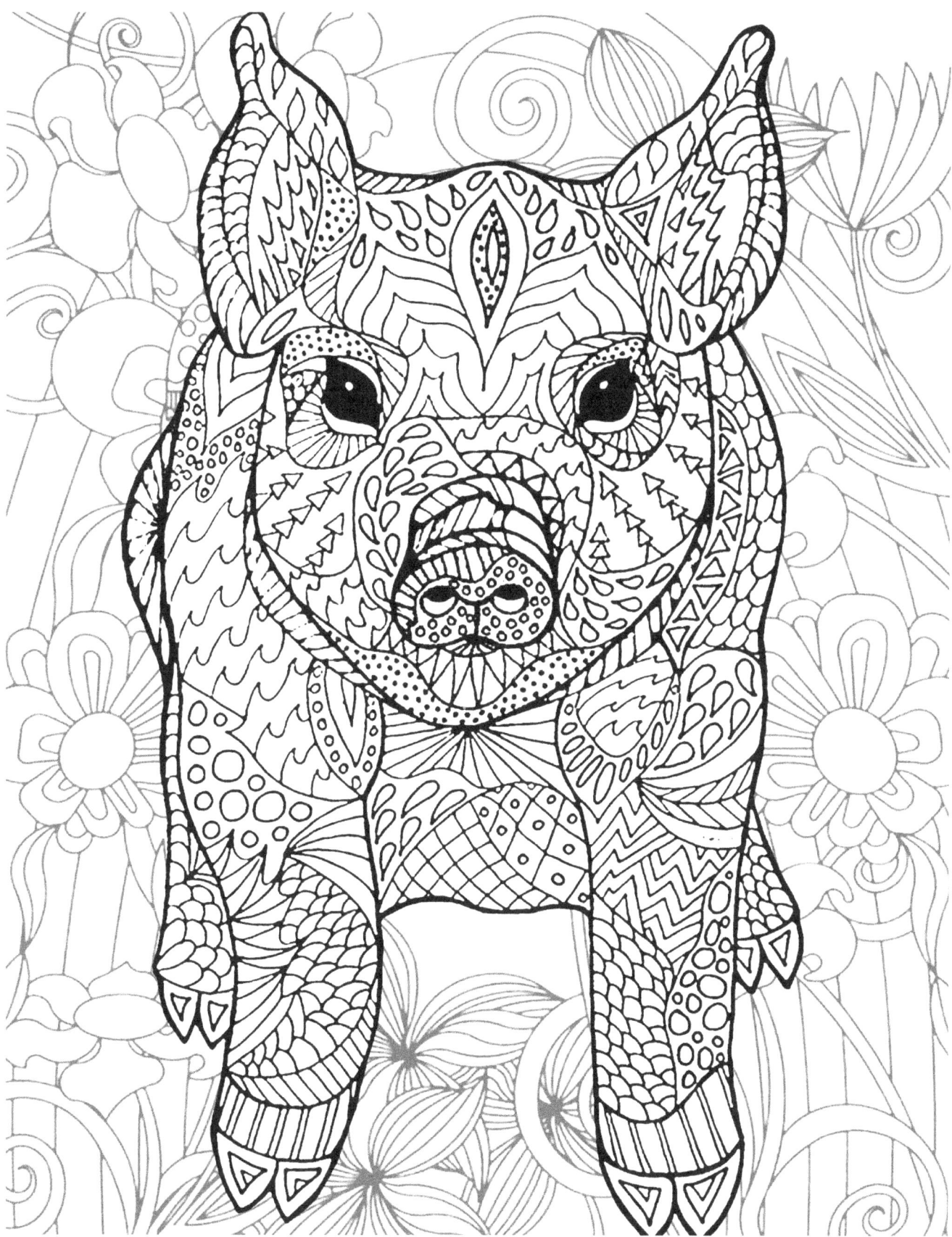

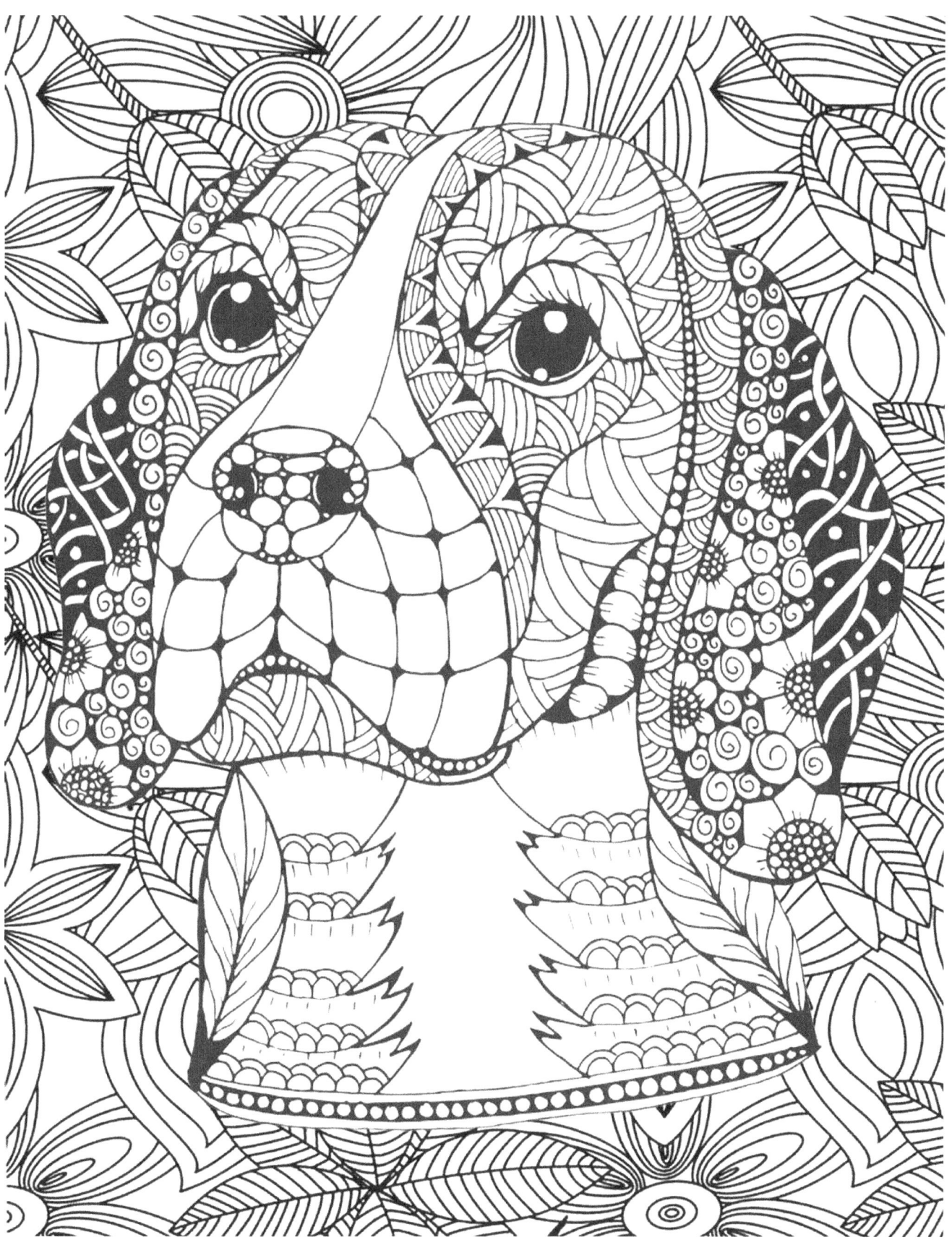

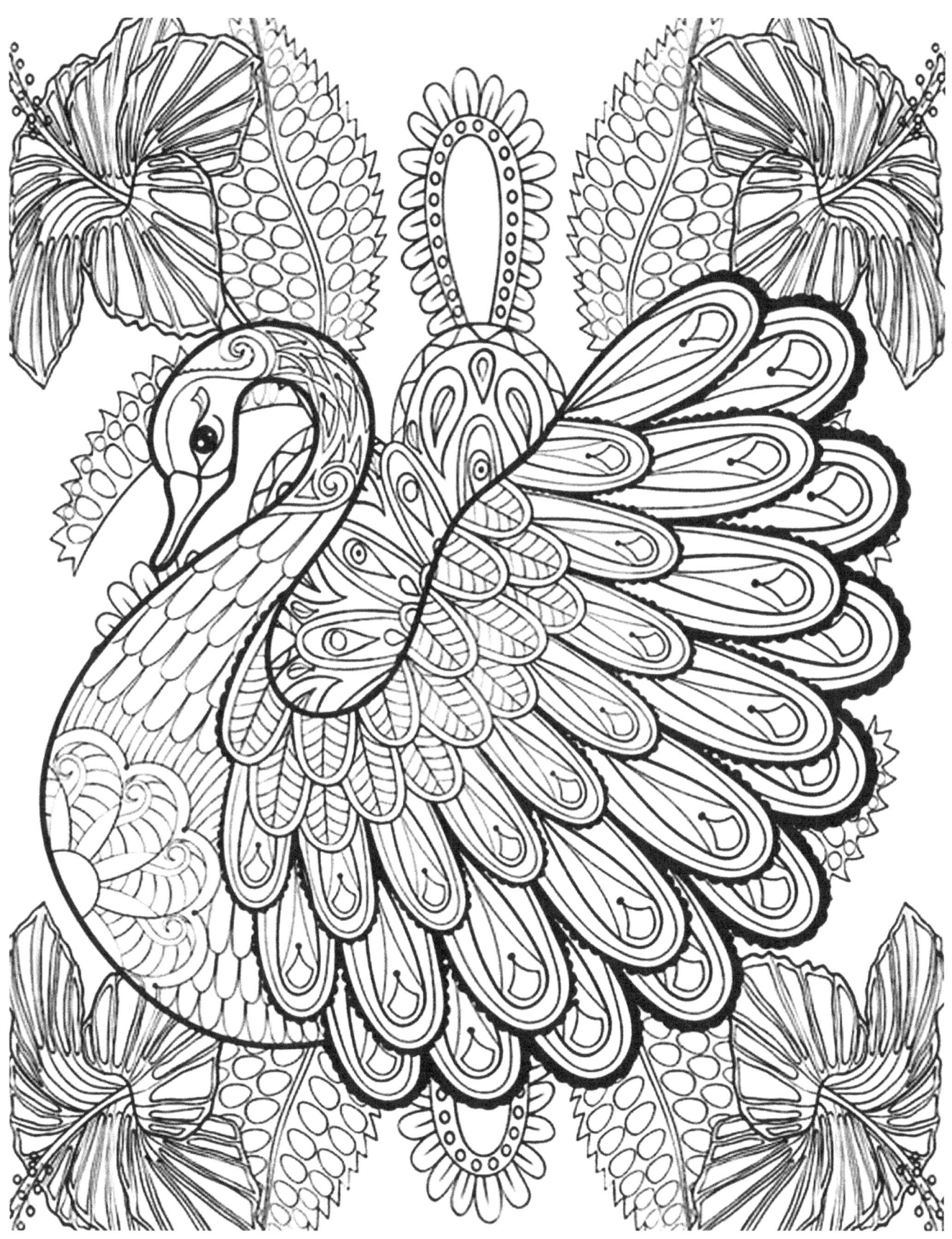

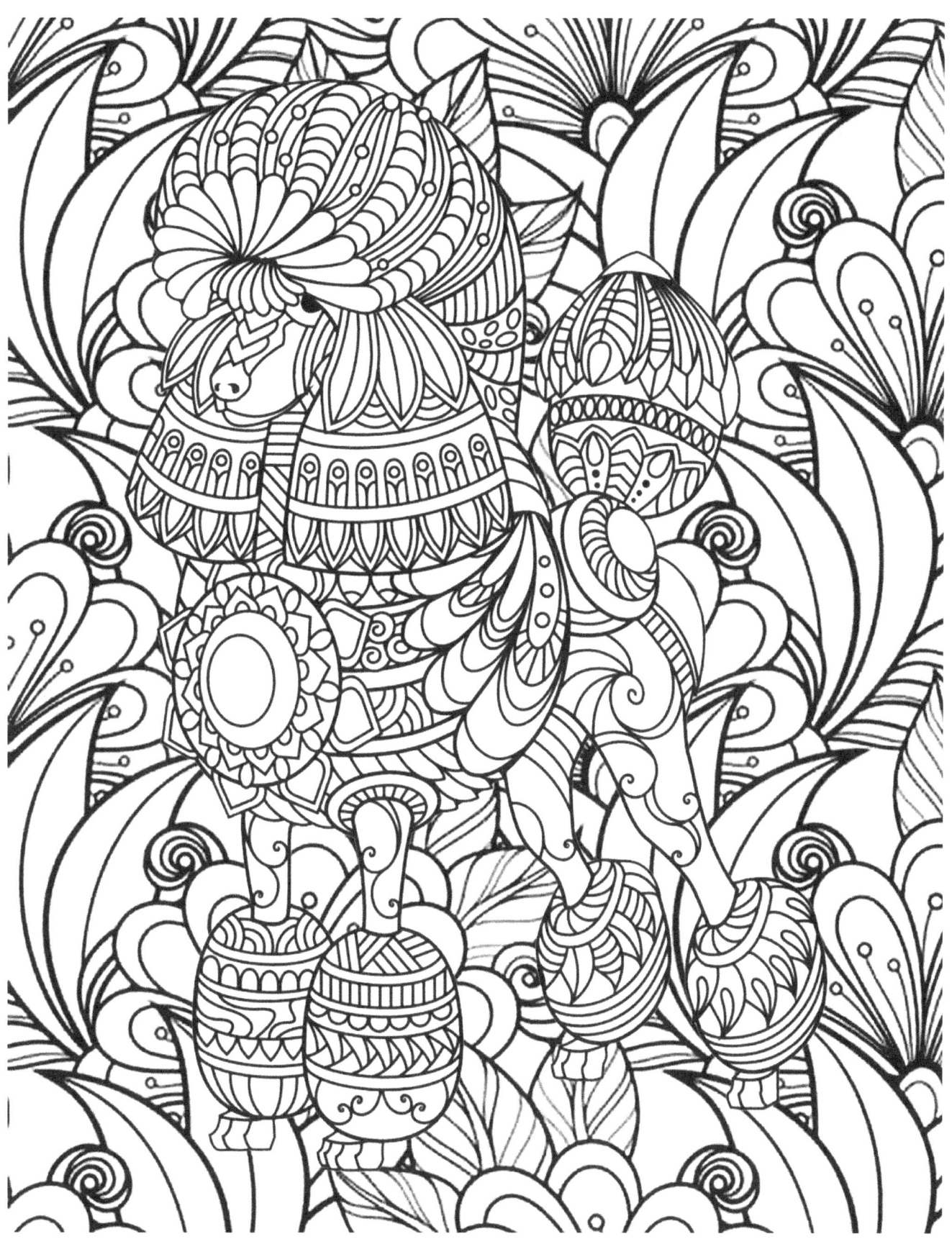

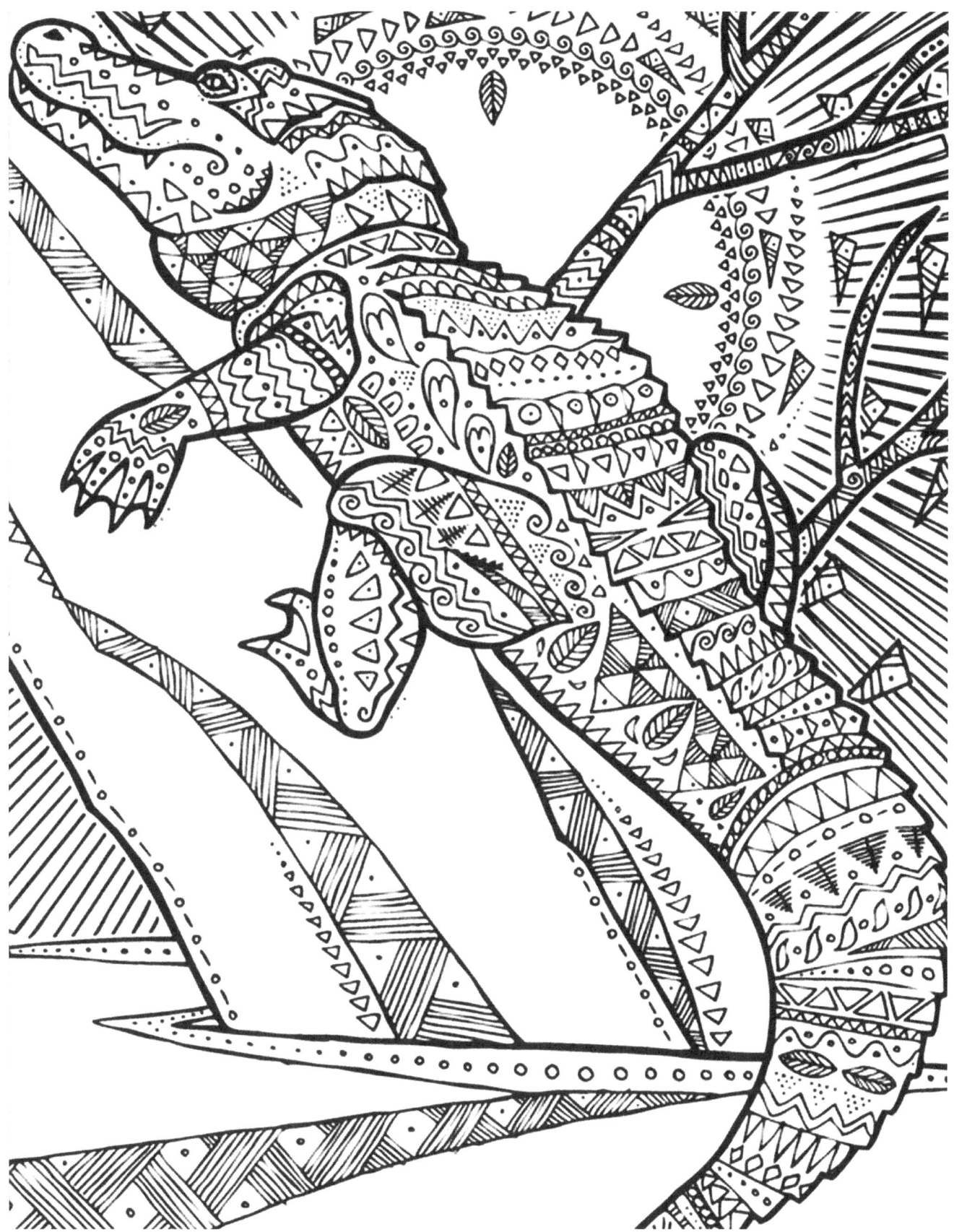

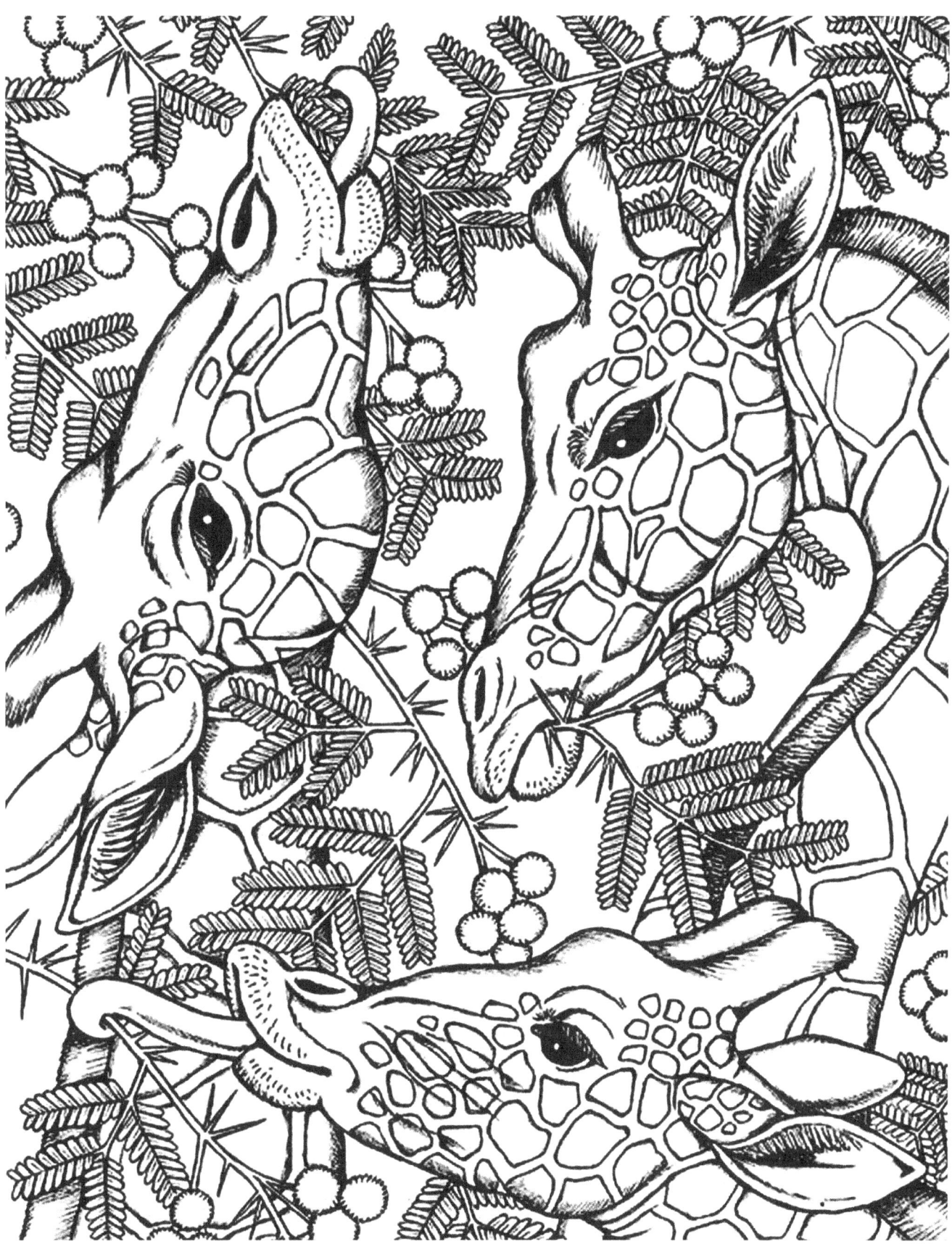

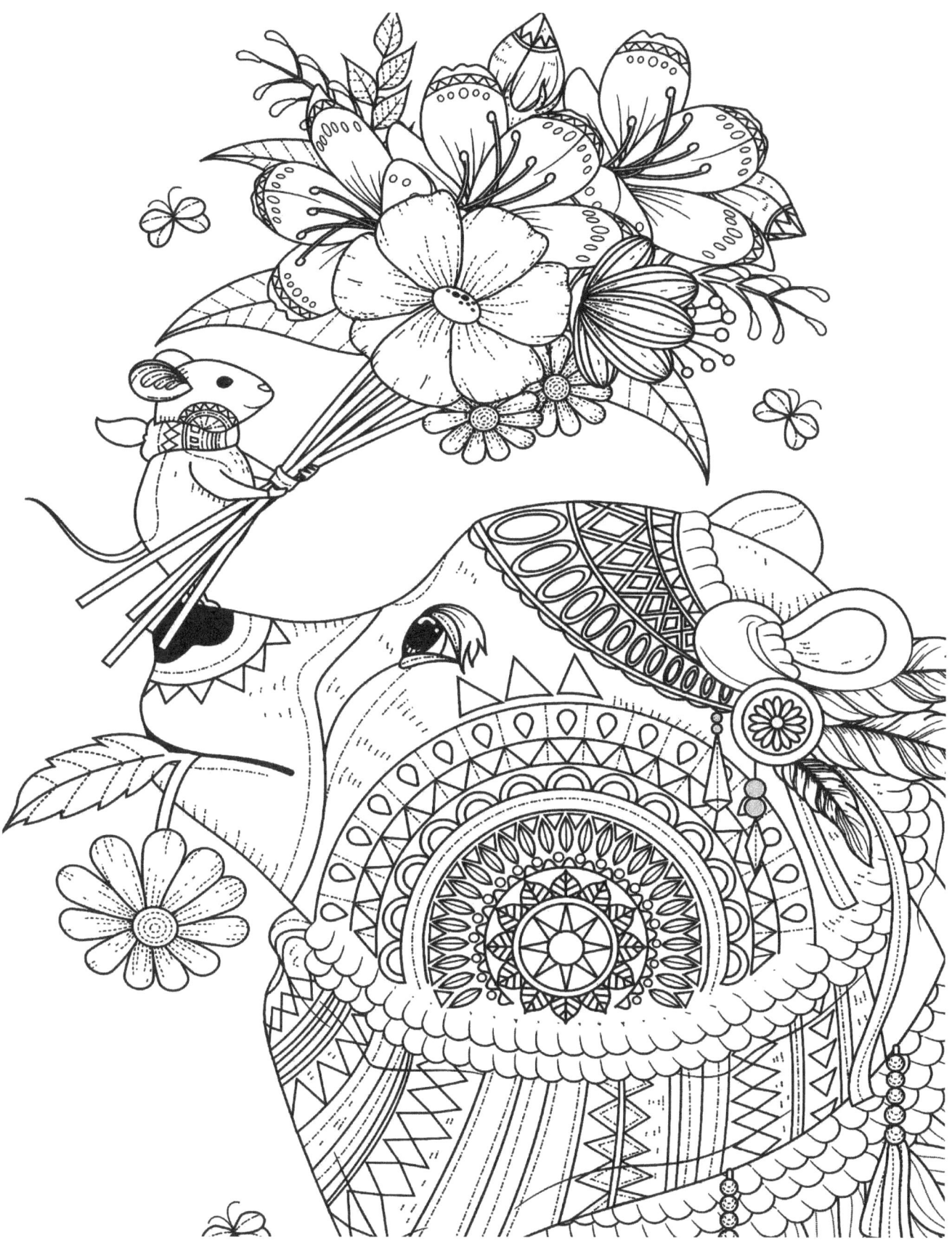

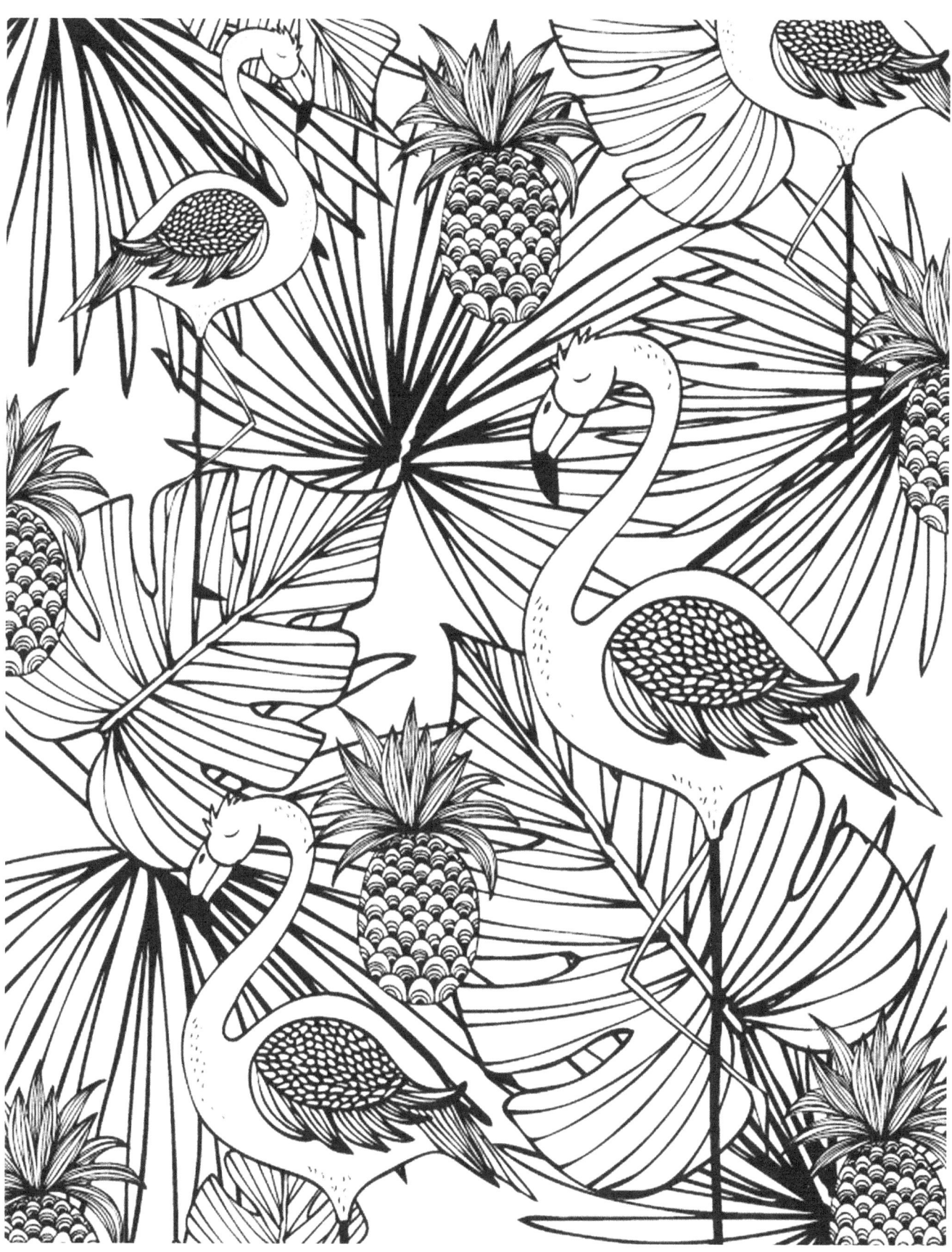

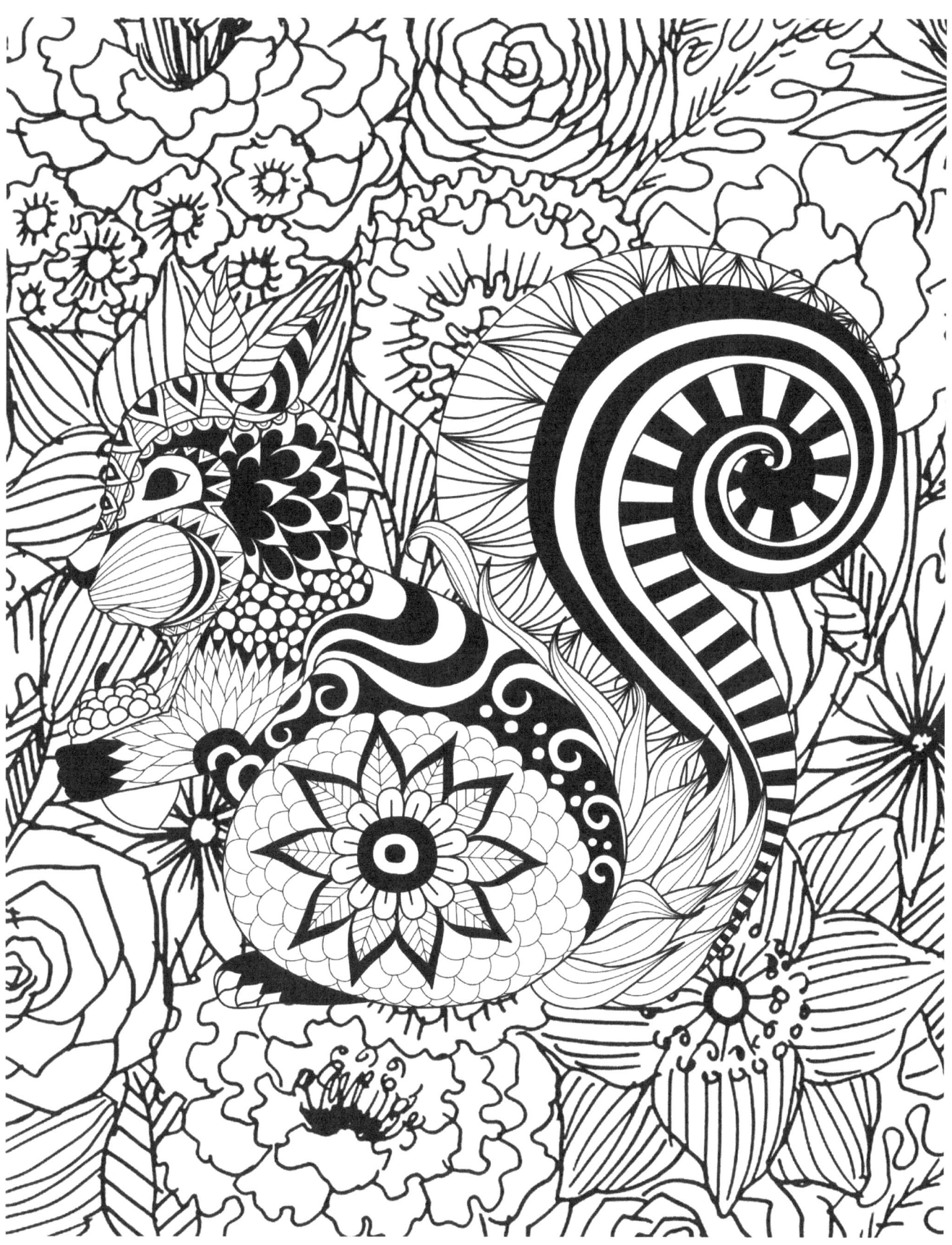

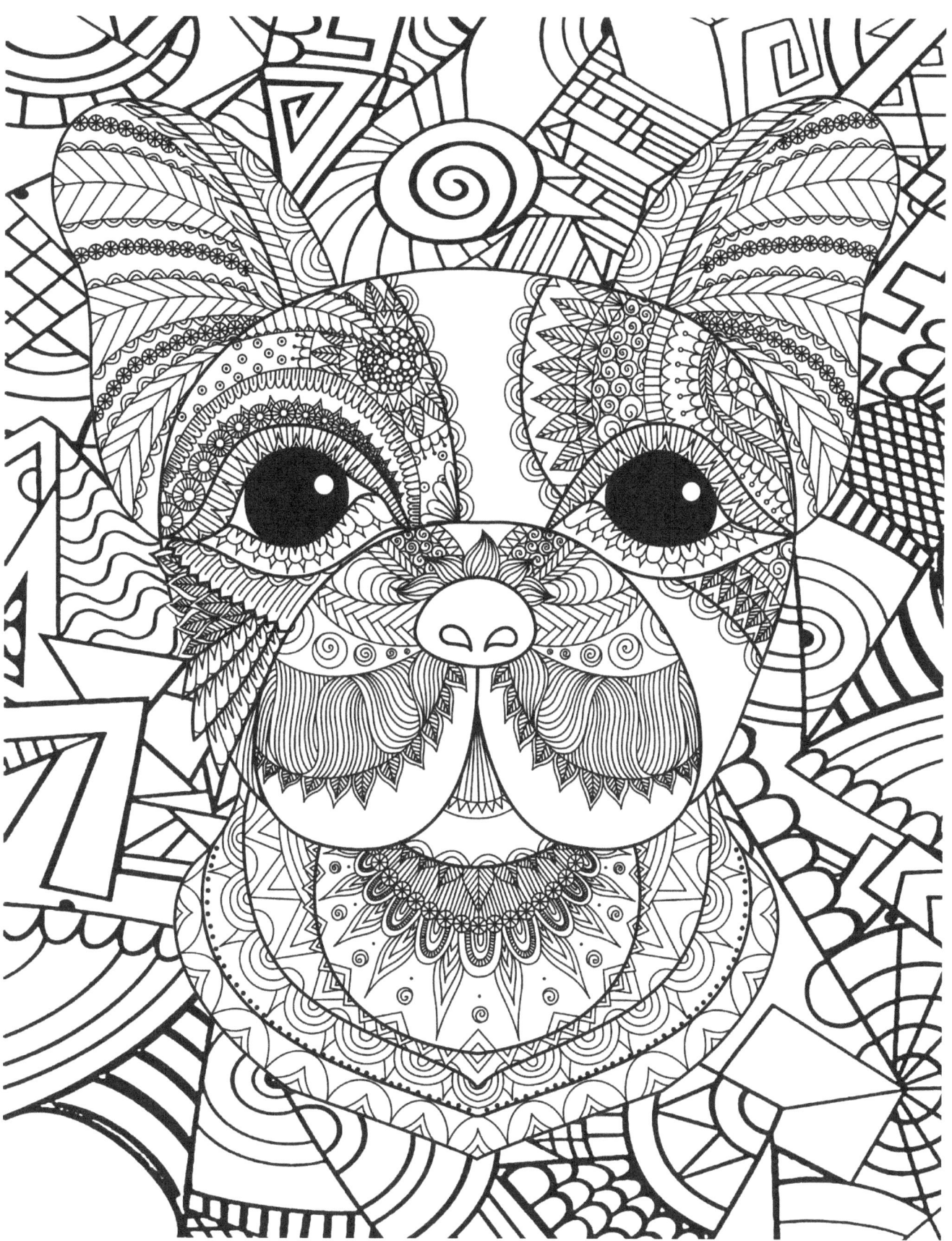

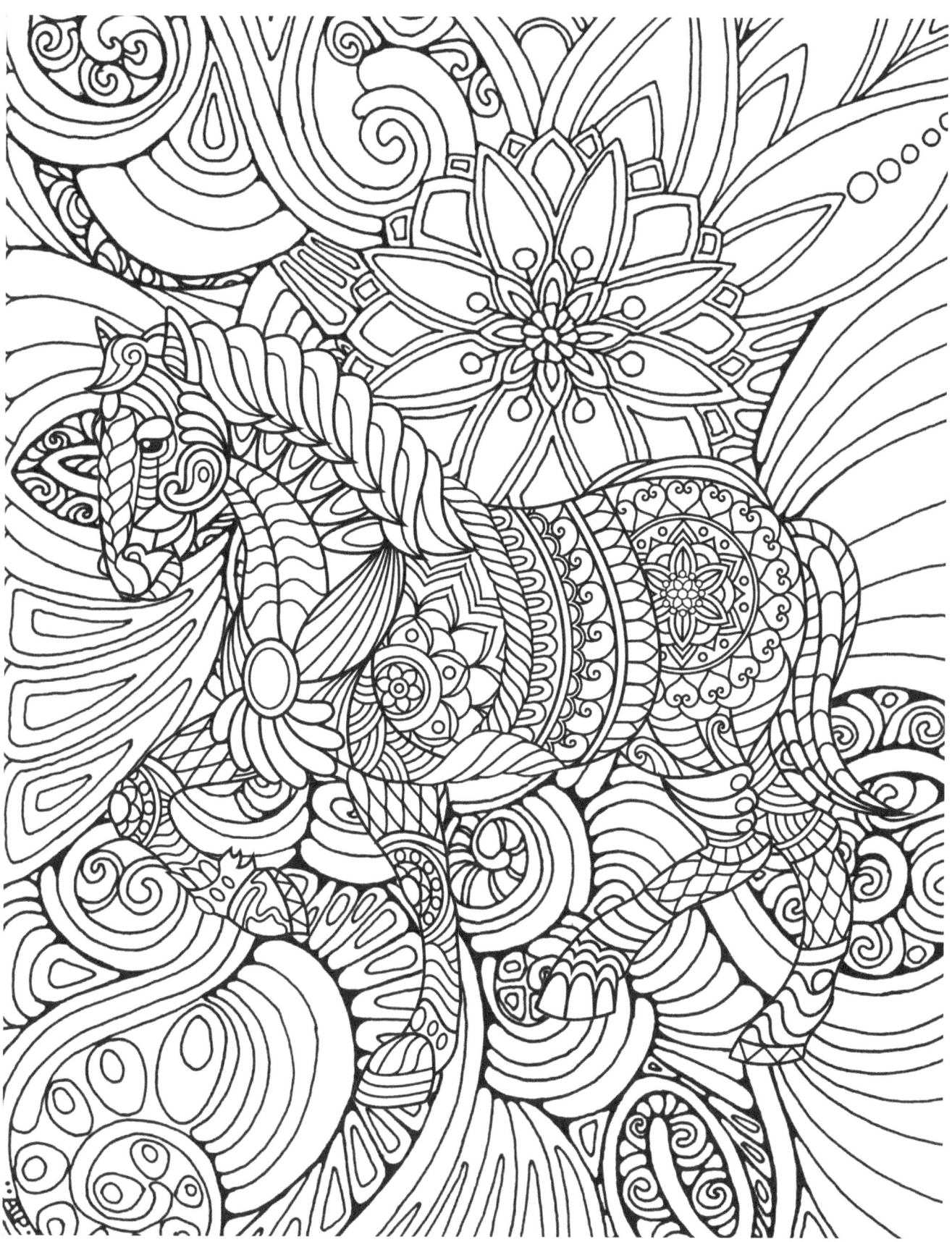

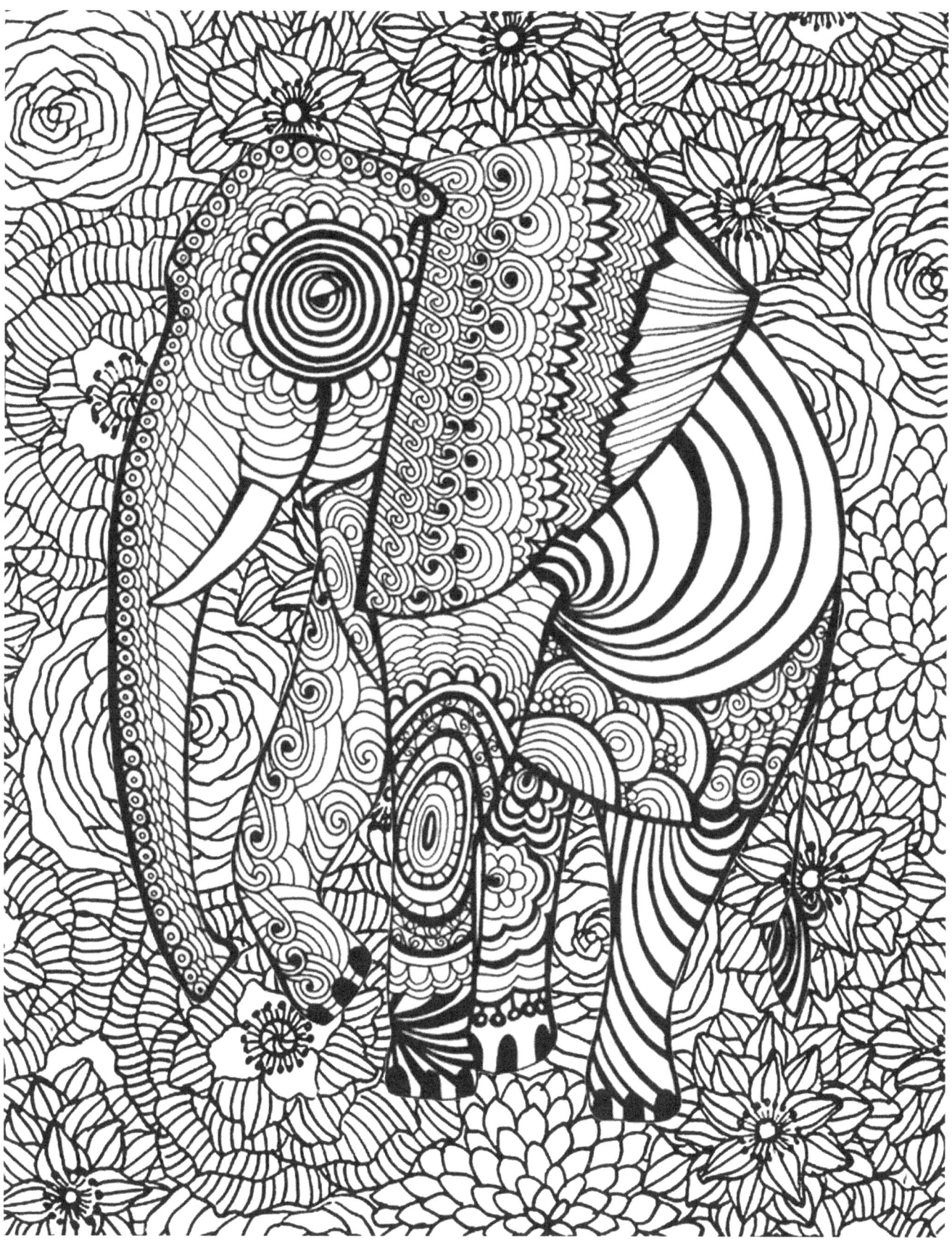

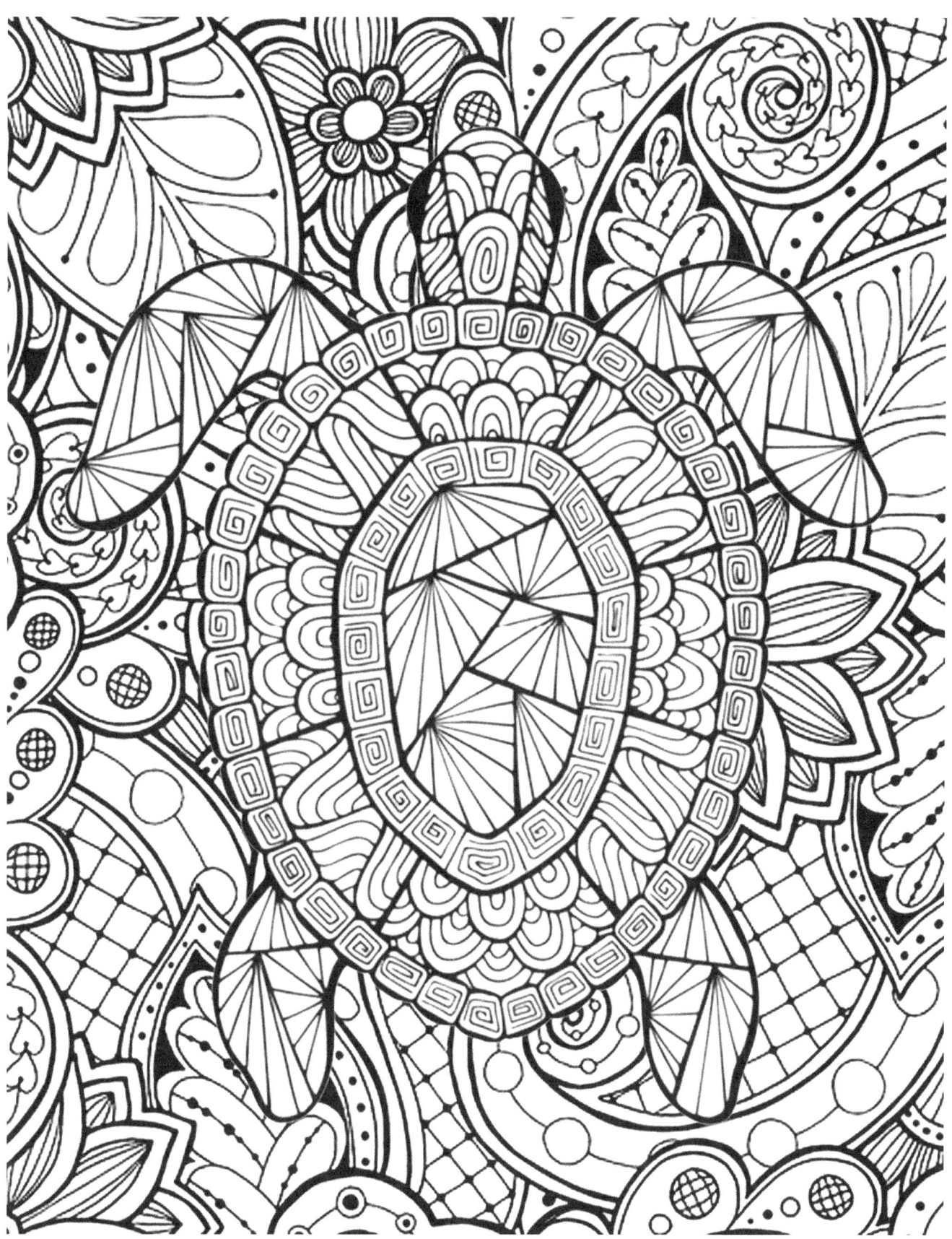

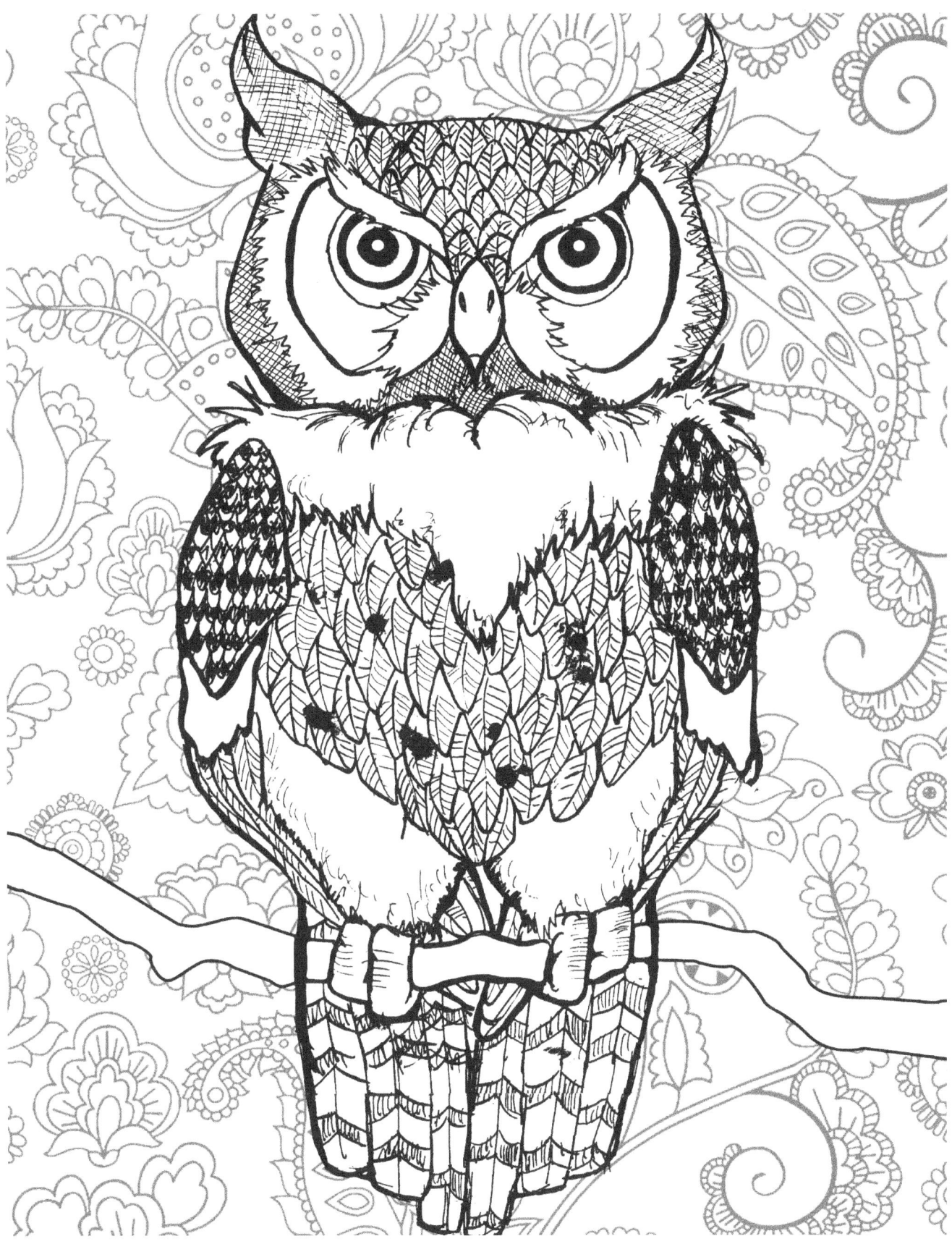

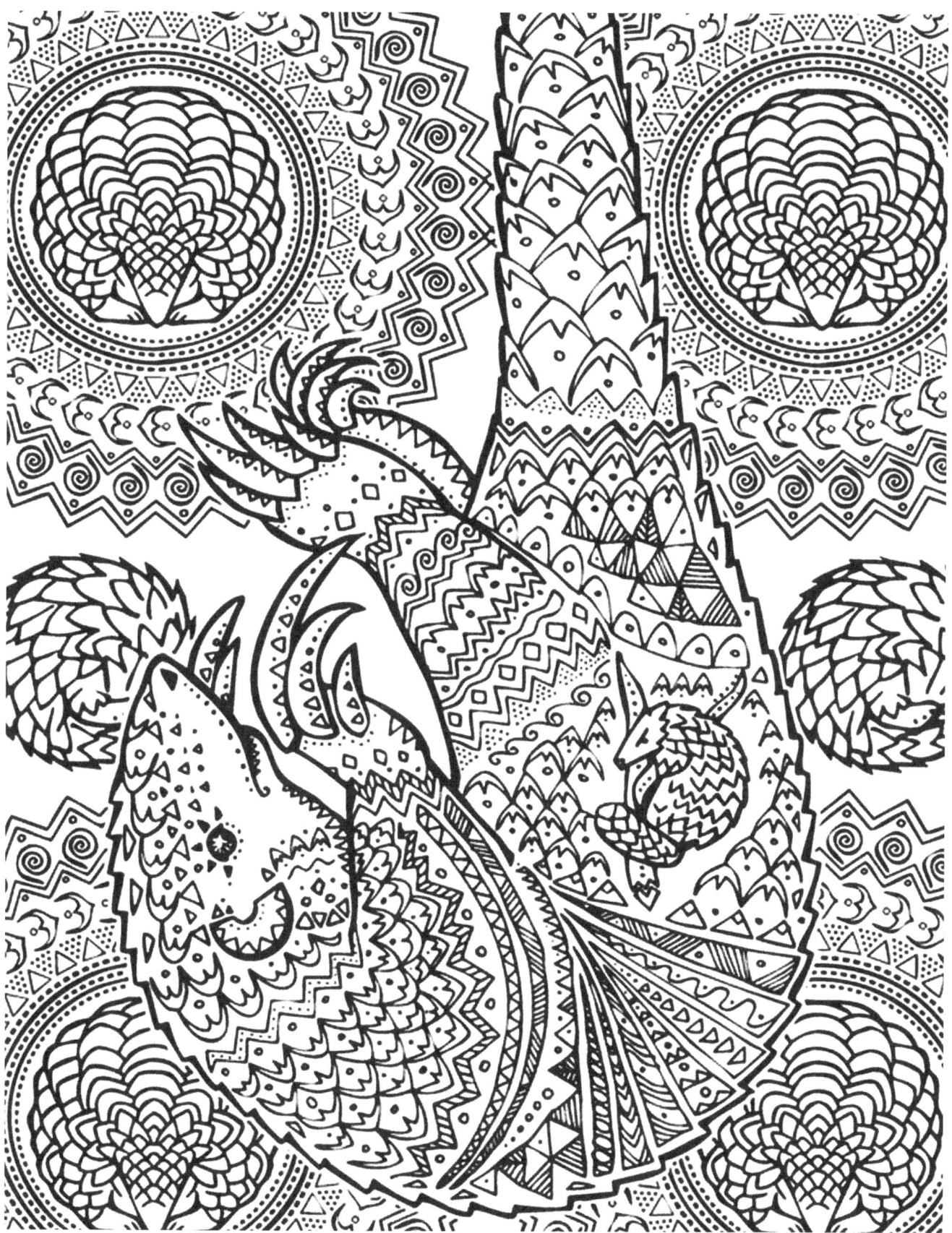

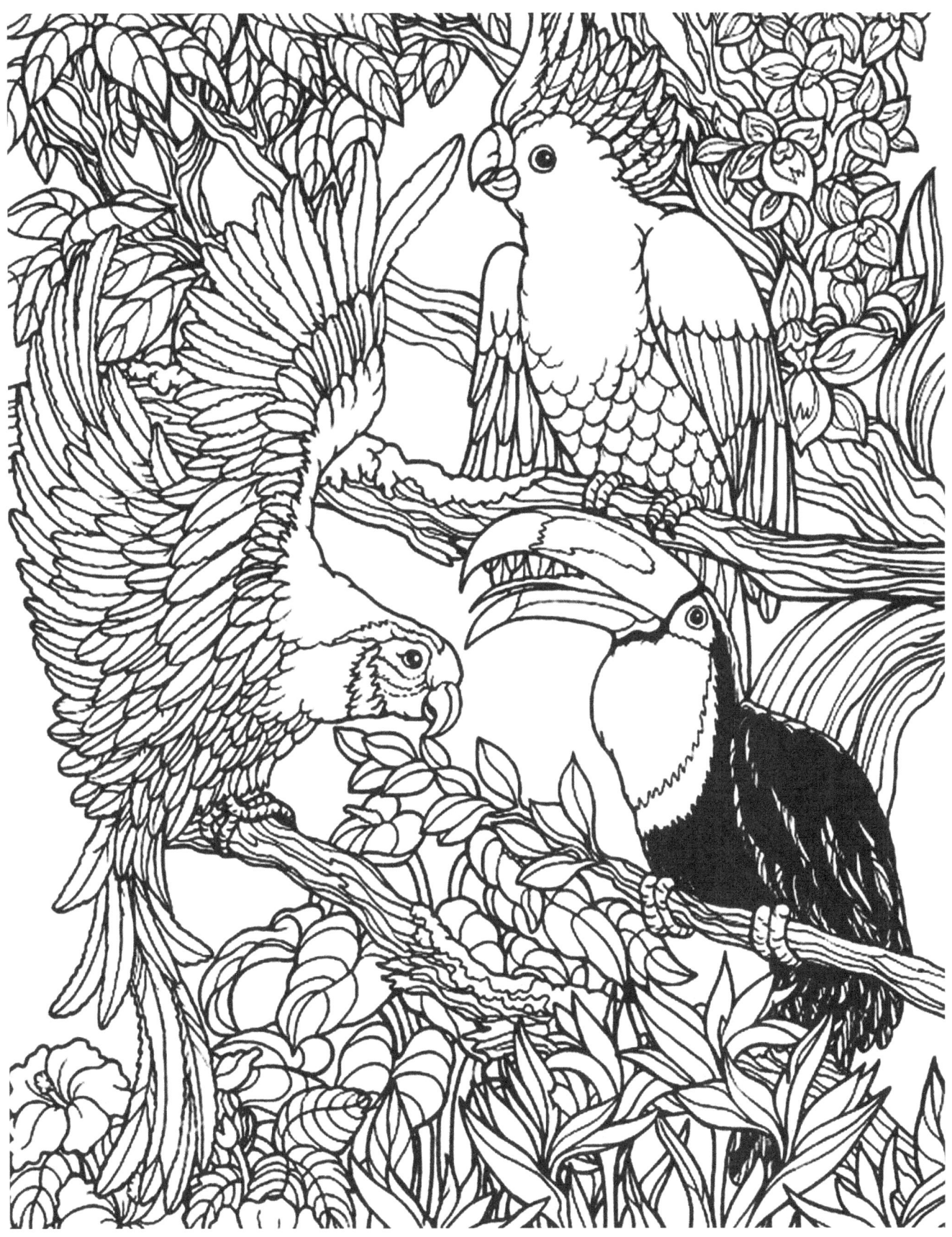